AUTHENTIC TRANSCRIPTIONS
WITH NOTES AND TABLATURE

Music transcriptions by Jeff Jacobson and Jeff Story

ISBN 0-634-05167-9

7777 W. Bluemound Rd. P.O. Box 13819 Milwaukee, WI 53213

In Australia Contact:
Hal Leonard Australia Pty. Ltd.
22 Taunton Drive P.O. Box 5130
Cheltenham East, 3192 Victoria, Australia
Email: ausadmin@halleonard.com

Visit Hal Leonard Online at
www.halleonard.com

I Feel So

Words and Music by Tom De Longe and Travis Barker

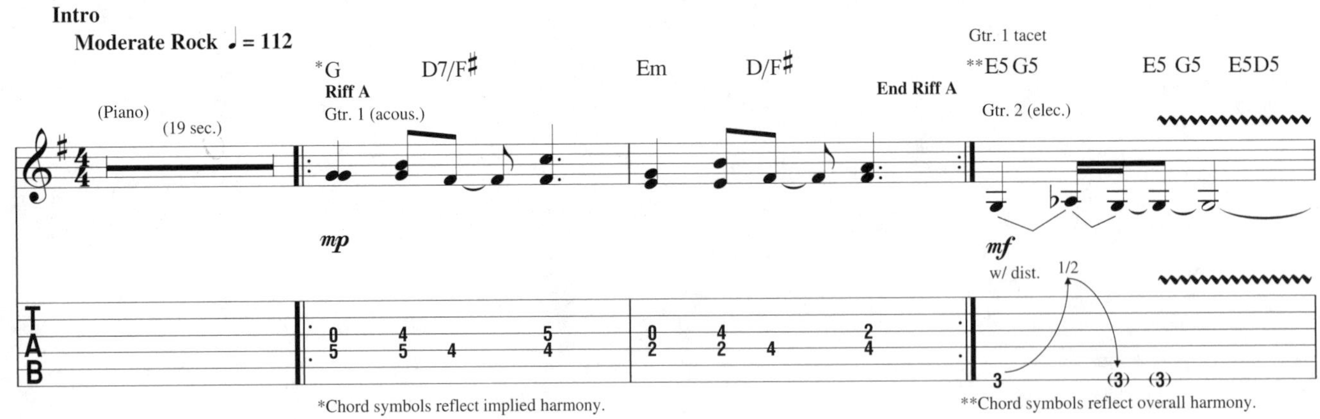

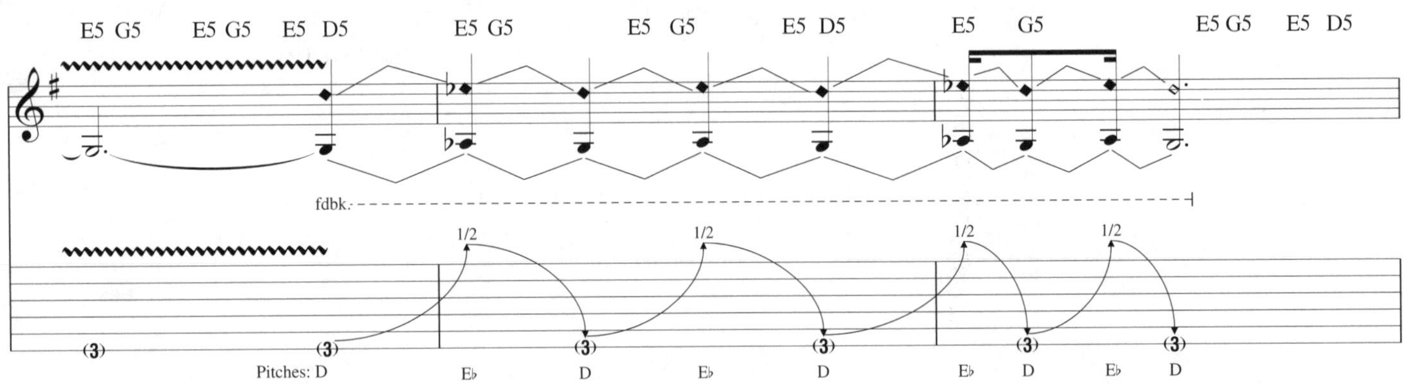

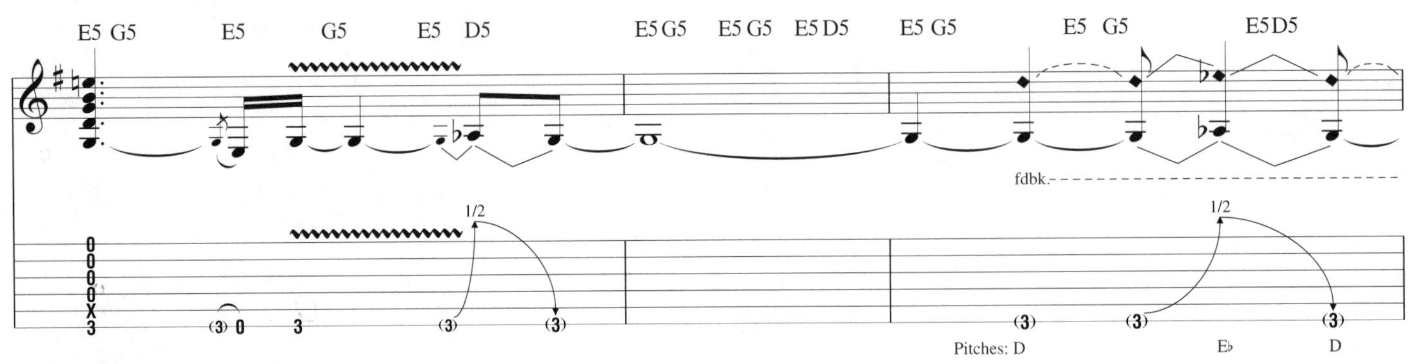

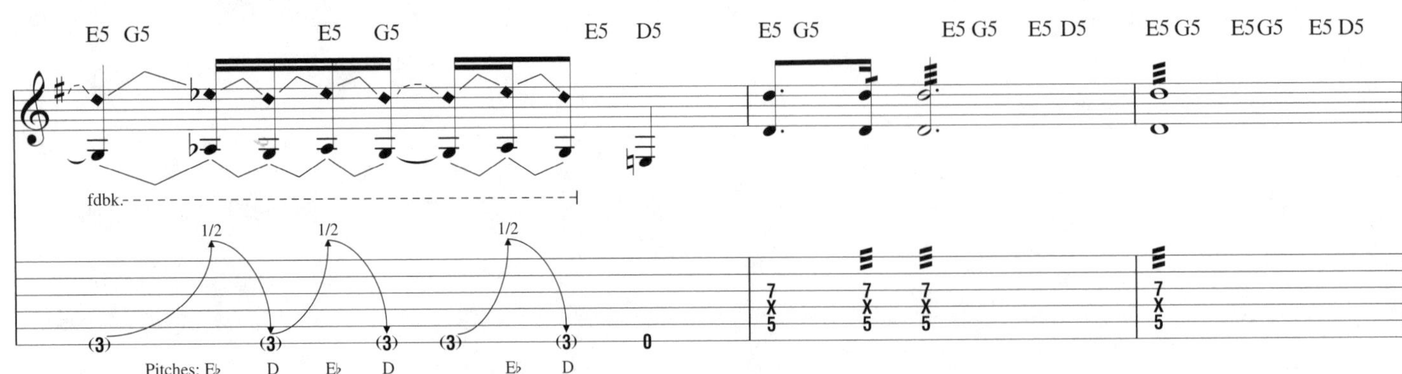

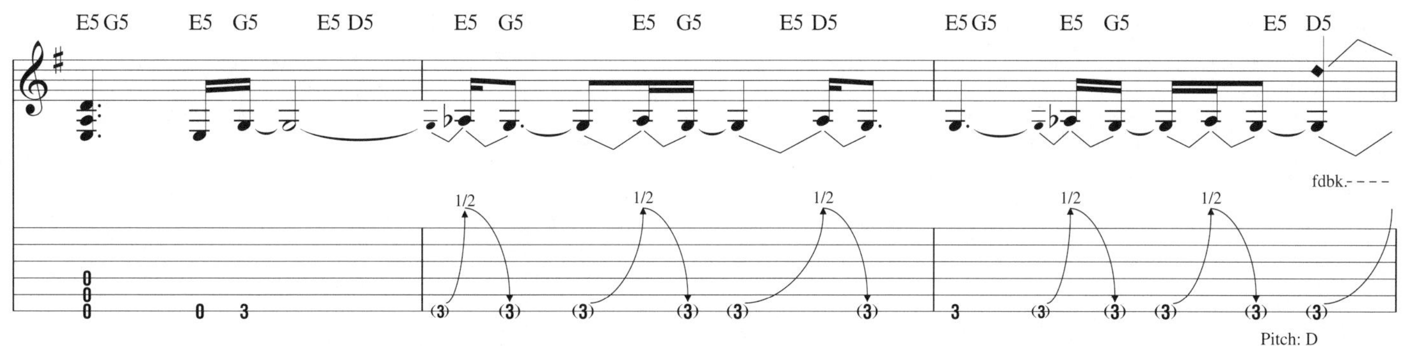
E5 G5
E5 G5
E5 D5
E5 G5
E5 G5
E5 D5
E5 G5
E5 G5
E5 D5
fdbk.
1/2
Pitch: D

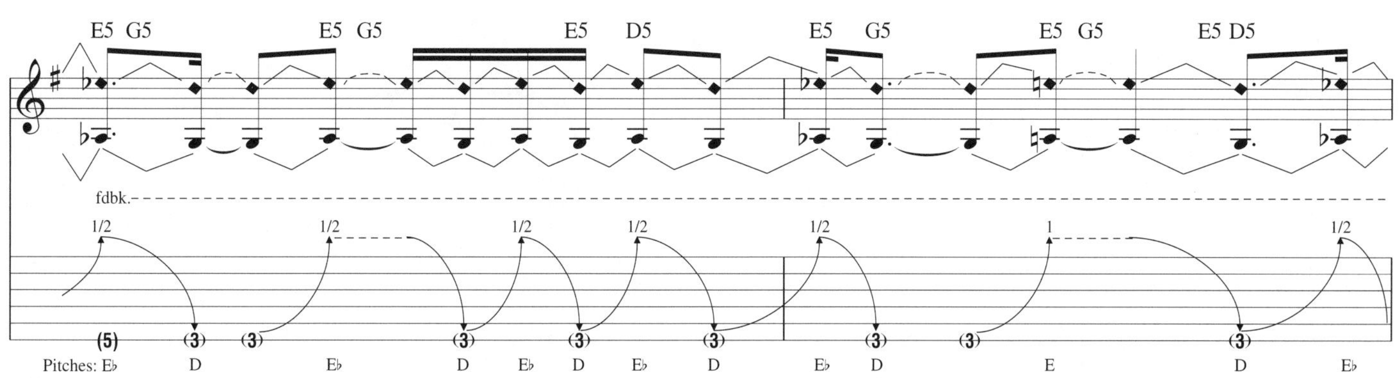
E5 G5
E5 G5
E5 D5
E5 G5
E5 G5
E5 D5
fdbk.
1/2
1
Pitches: E♭ D E♭ D E♭ D E♭ D E♭ D E D E♭

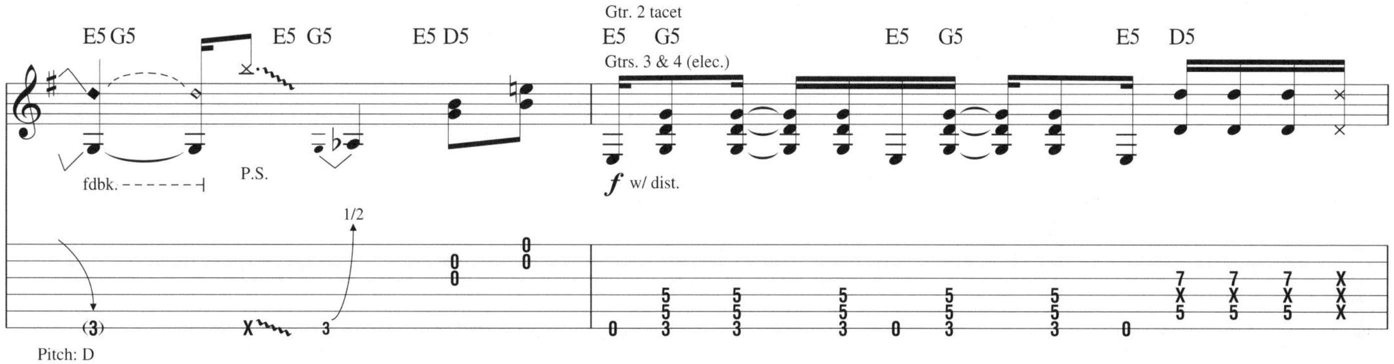
E5 G5
E5 G5
E5 D5
Gtr. 2 tacet
E5 G5
Gtrs. 3 & 4 (elec.)
E5 G5
E5 D5
fdbk.
P.S.
f w/ dist.
1/2
Pitch: D

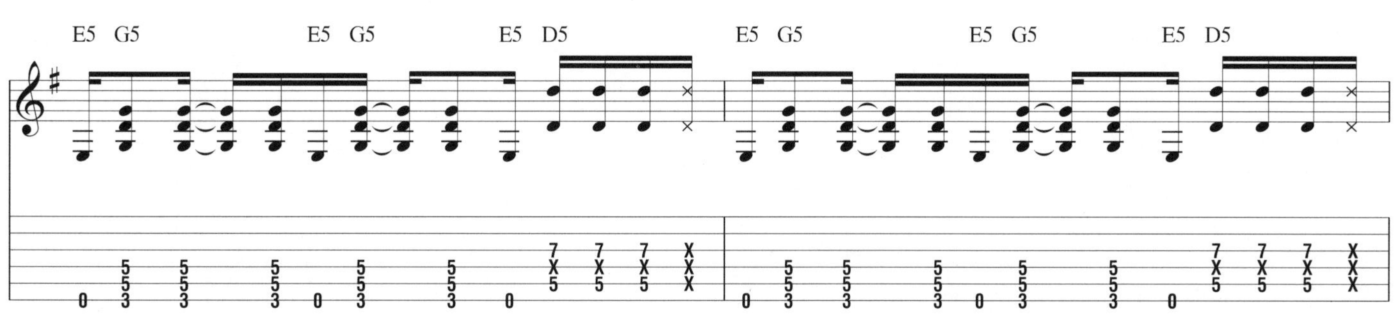
E5 G5
E5 G5
E5 D5
E5 G5
E5 G5
E5 D5

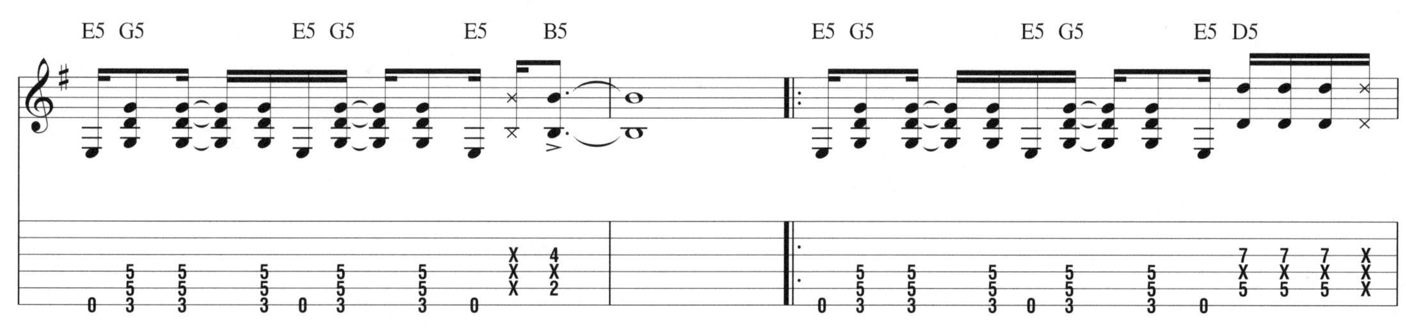
E5 G5
E5 G5
E5
B5
E5 G5
E5 G5
E5 D5

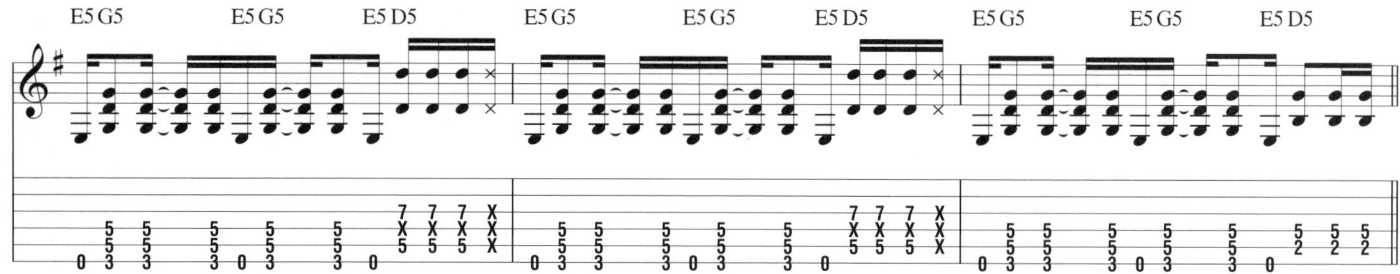

Verse

Gtr. 1: w/ Riff A (4 times)
Gtrs. 3 & 4 tacet

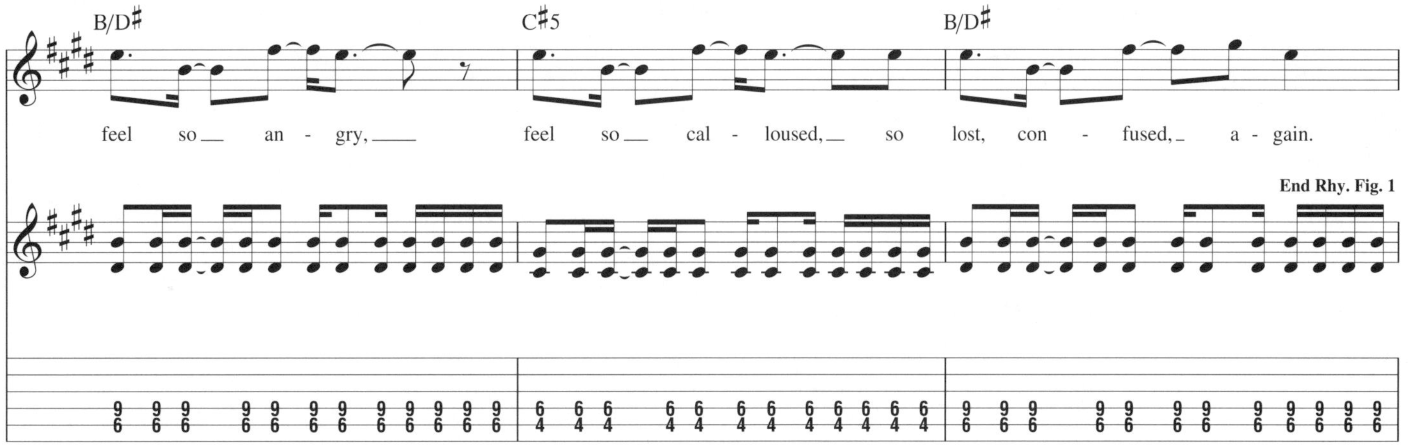
B/D#
C#5
B/D#
feel so__ an - gry,____ feel so__ cal - loused,__ so lost, con - fused,_ a - gain.
End Rhy. Fig. 1

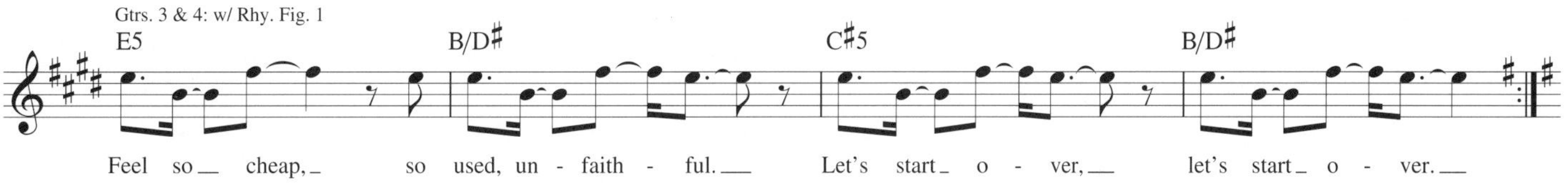
Gtrs. 3 & 4: w/ Rhy. Fig. 1
E5
B/D#
C#5
B/D#
Feel so__ cheap,_ so used, un - faith - ful.___ Let's start_ o - ver,___ let's start_ o - ver.___

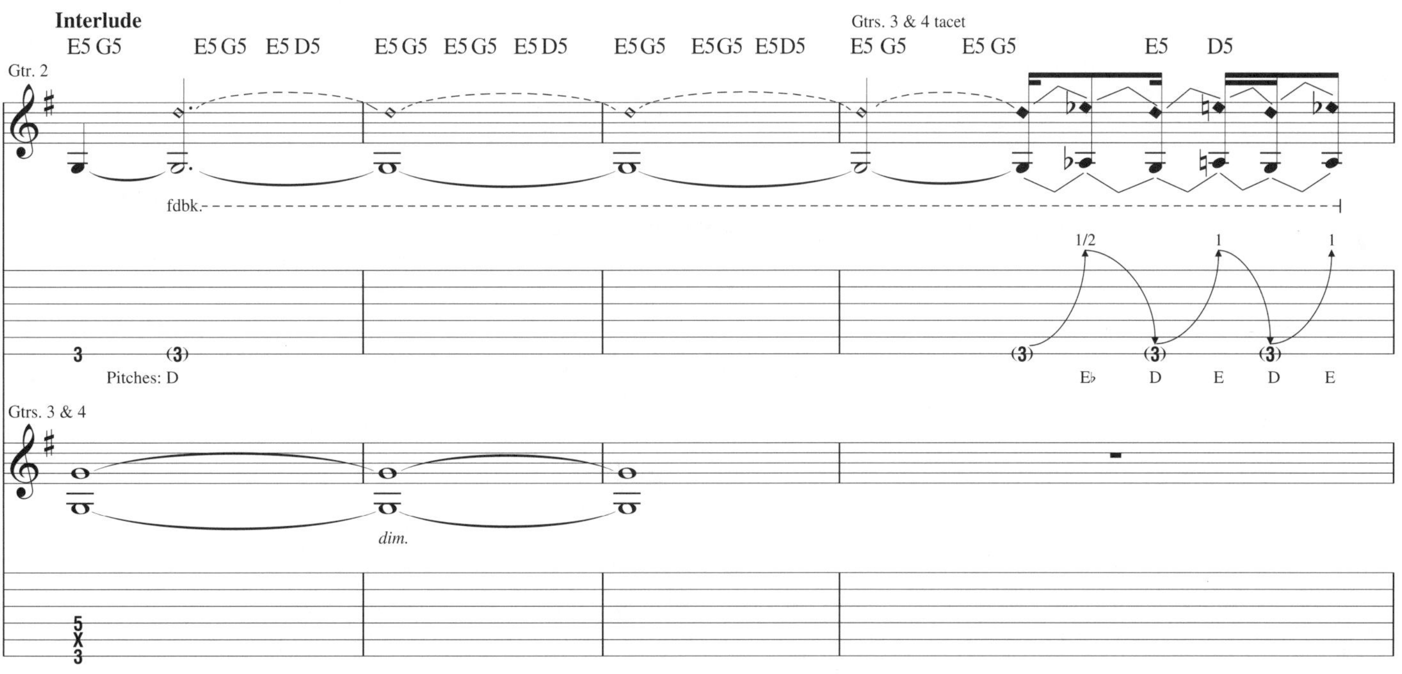
Interlude
Gtr. 2
fdbk.
Pitches: D
Gtrs. 3 & 4
dim.
Gtrs. 3 & 4 tacet

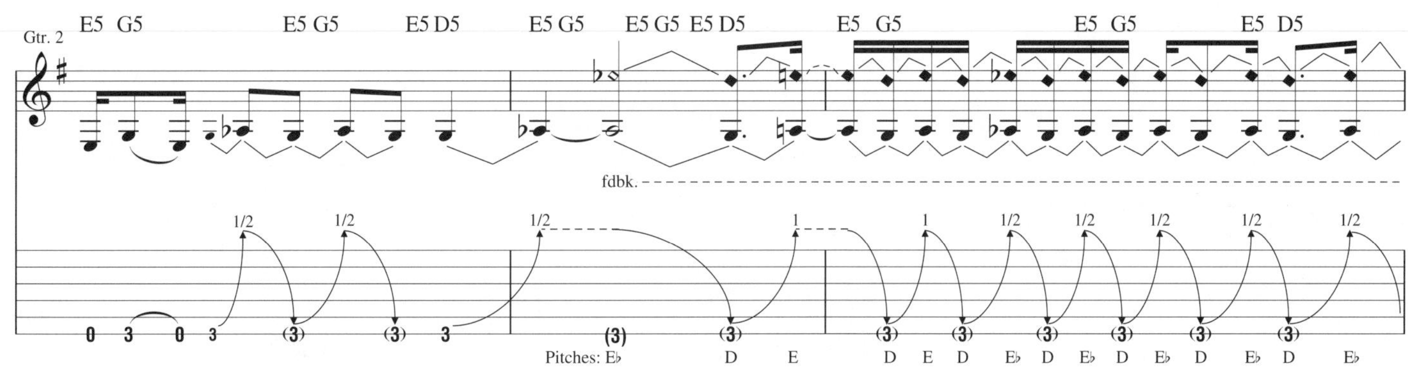
Gtr. 2
fdbk.
Pitches: E♭

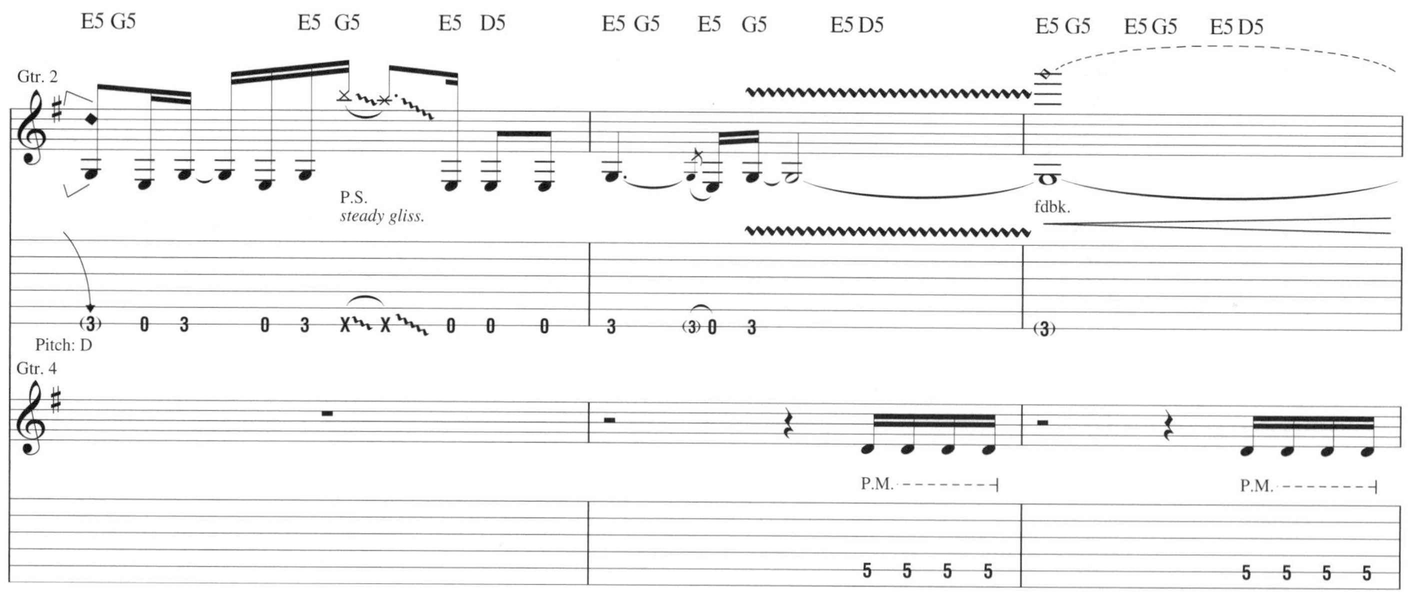
E5 G5
E5 G5
E5 D5
E5 G5
E5 G5
E5 D5
E5 G5
E5 G5
E5 D5
Gtr. 2
P.S.
steady gliss.
fdbk.
Pitch: D
Gtr. 4
P.M.
P.M.

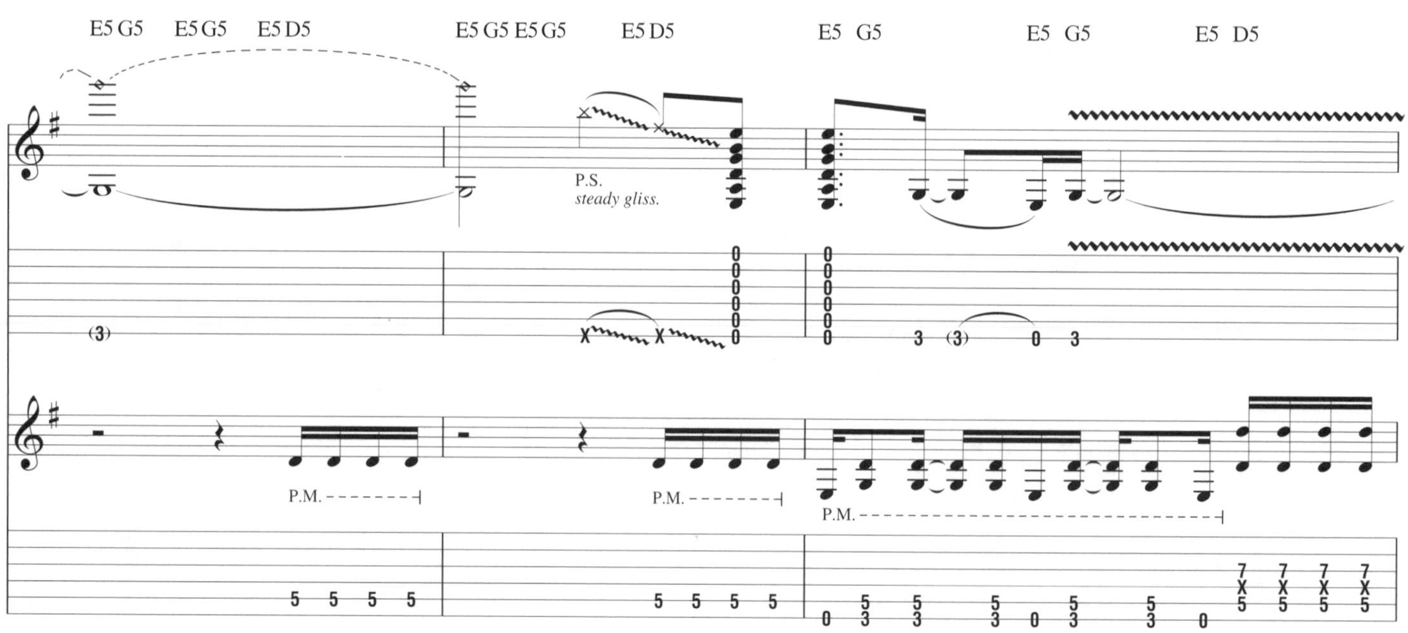
E5 G5
E5 G5
E5 D5
E5 G5 E5 G5
E5 D5
E5 G5
E5 G5
E5 D5
P.S.
steady gliss.
P.M.
P.M.
P.M.

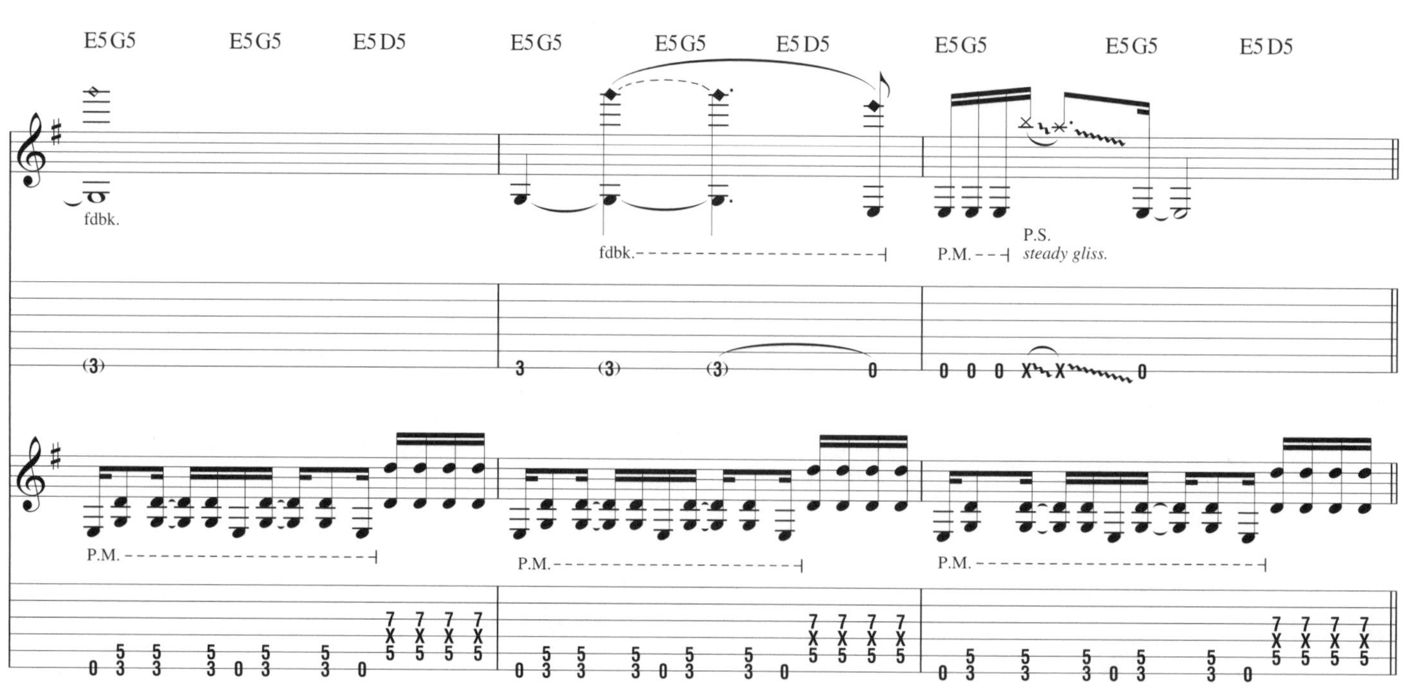
E5 G5
E5 G5
E5 D5
E5 G5
E5 G5
E5 D5
E5 G5
E5 G5
E5 D5
fdbk.
fdbk.
P.M.
P.S.
steady gliss.
P.M.
P.M.
P.M.

Gtr. 2 tacet
B5
Gtrs. 3 & 4

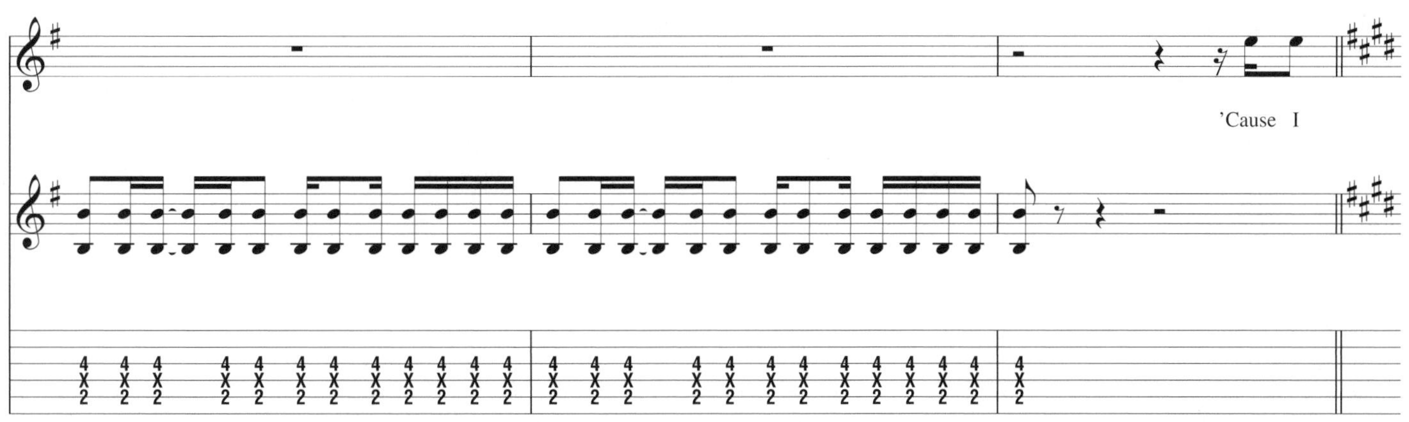
'Cause I

Chorus

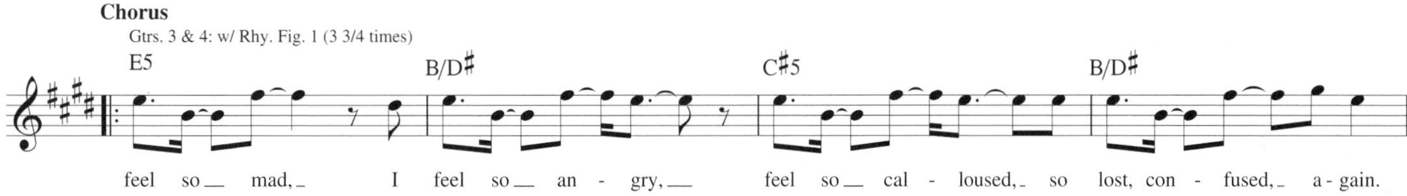
Gtrs. 3 & 4: w/ Rhy. Fig. 1 (3 3/4 times)
E5
B/D♯
C♯5
B/D♯
feel so mad, I feel so an - gry, feel so cal - loused, so lost, con - fused, a - gain.

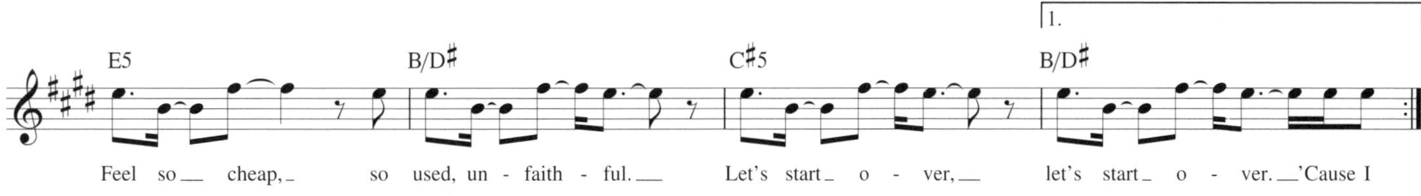
1.
E5
B/D♯
C♯5
B/D♯
Feel so cheap, so used, un - faith - ful. Let's start o - ver, let's start o - ver. 'Cause I

2.
B/D♯
Free time
E5
let's start o - ver. Let's start o - ver.
Gtrs. 3 & 4

All Systems Go

Words and Music by Tom De Longe and Travis Barker

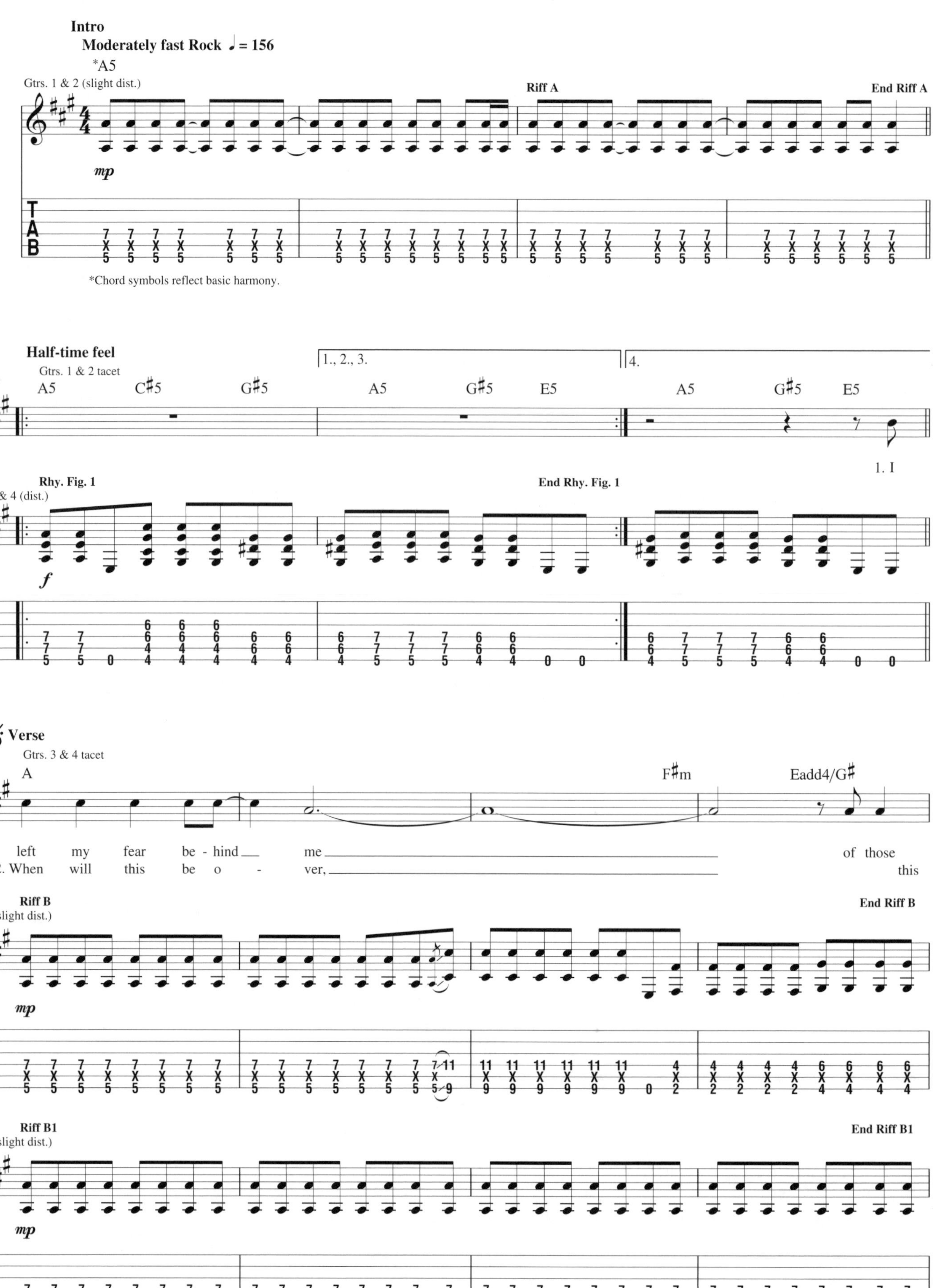

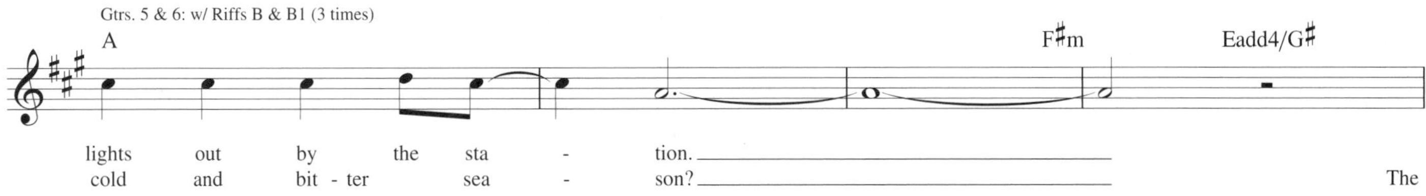
Gtrs. 5 & 6: w/ Riffs B & B1 (3 times)
A
F♯m
Eadd4/G♯
lights out by the sta - tion.
cold and bit - ter sea - son?
The

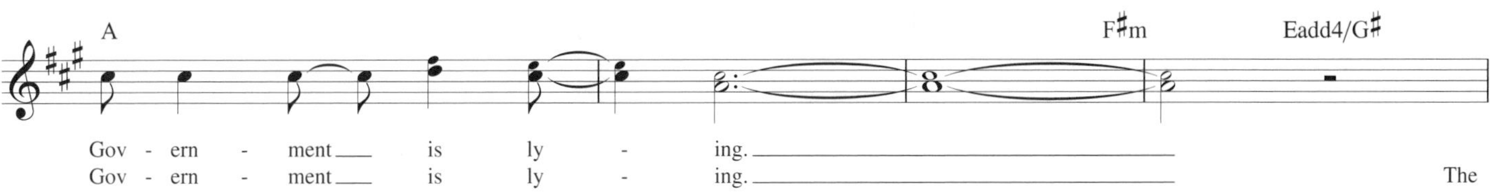
A
F♯m
Eadd4/G♯
Gov - ern - ment is ly - ing.
Gov - ern - ment is ly - ing.
The

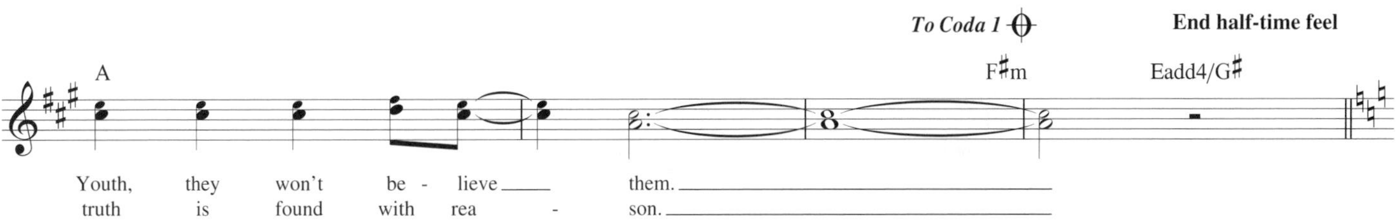
To Coda 1
End half-time feel
A
F♯m
Eadd4/G♯
Youth, they won't be - lieve them.
truth is found with rea - son.

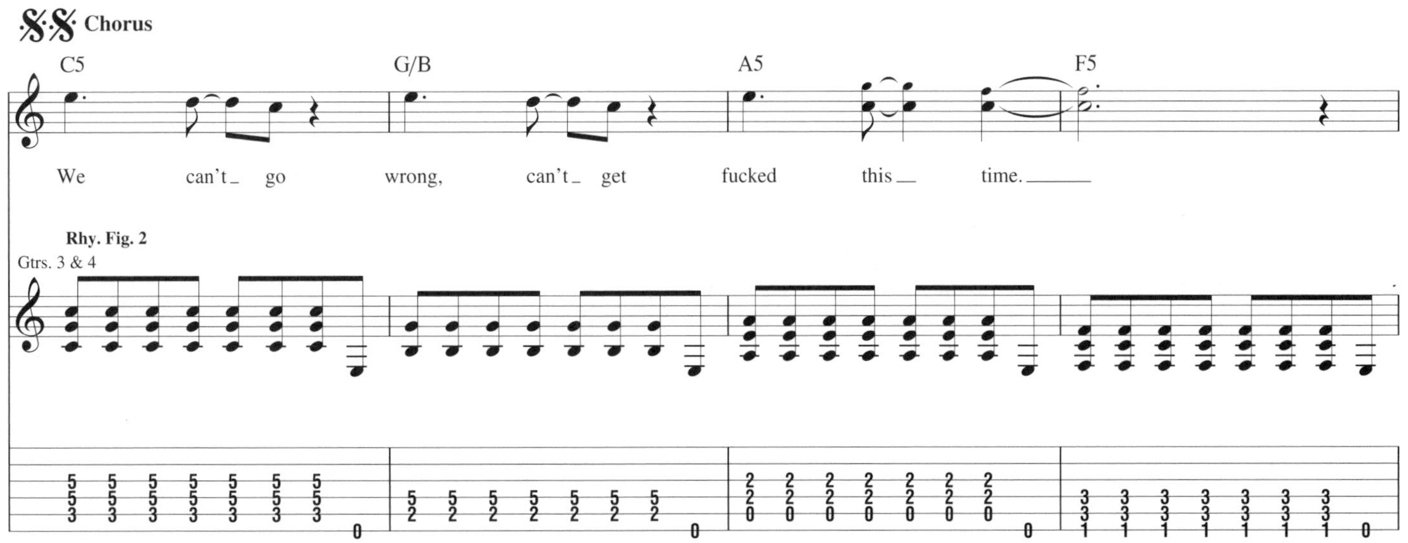
Chorus
C5
G/B
A5
F5
We can't go wrong, can't get fucked this time.
Rhy. Fig. 2
Gtrs. 3 & 4

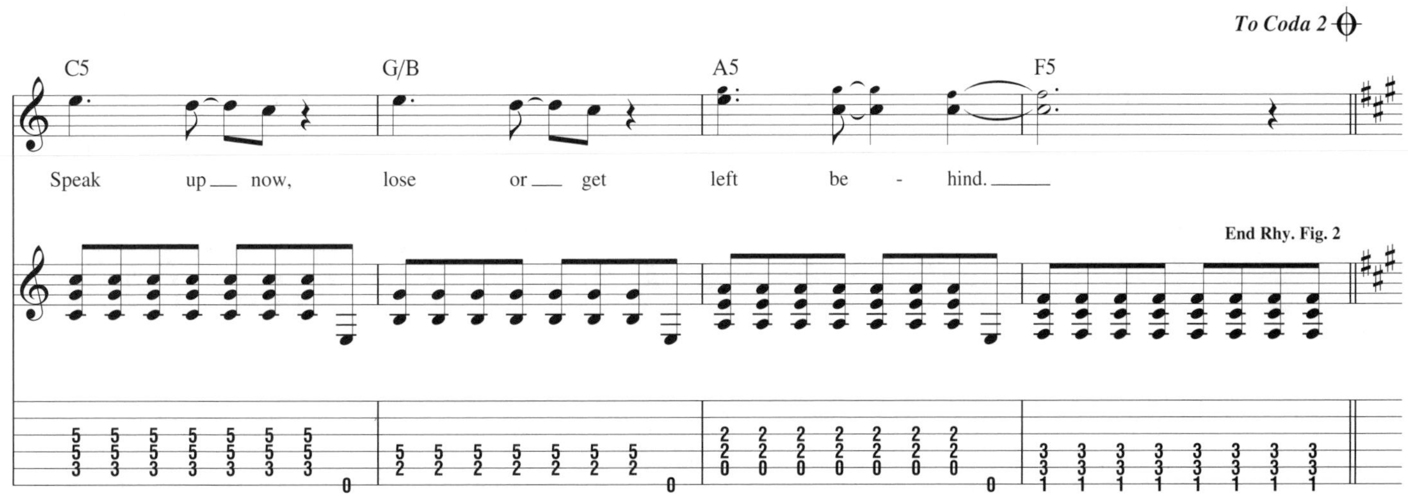
To Coda 2
C5
G/B
A5
F5
Speak up now, lose or get left be - hind.
End Rhy. Fig. 2

Interlude
2nd time, D.S. al Coda 1
Gtrs. 3 & 4 tacet
A5
Gtrs. 1 & 2
mf
Gtrs. 1 & 2 tacet
A5 C#m G#5 A5 G#5 E5
Gtrs. 3 & 4
f

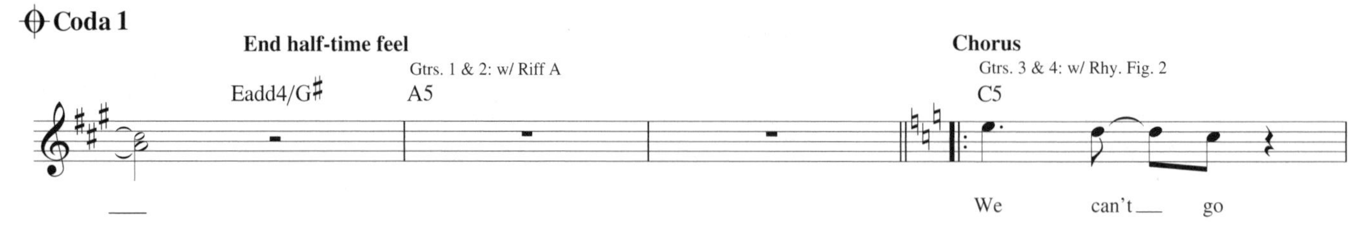
Coda 1
End half-time feel
Eadd4/G#
Gtrs. 1 & 2: w/ Riff A
A5
Chorus
Gtrs. 3 & 4: w/ Rhy. Fig. 2
C5
We can't go

G/B A5 F5 C5
wrong, can't get fucked this time. Speak up now,

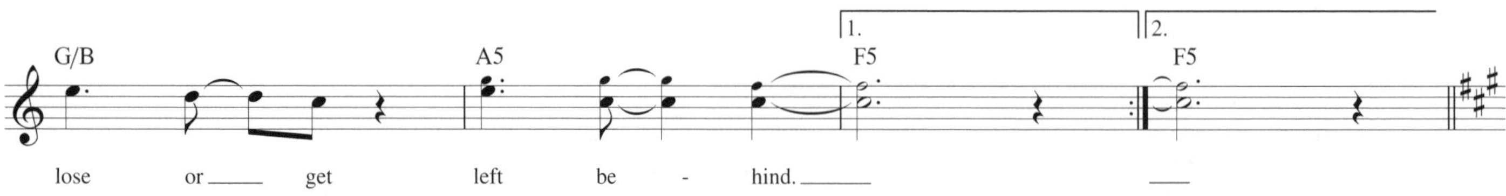
1.
2.
G/B A5 F5 F5
lose or get left be - hind.

Interlude
Gtr. 5
A5
1.,3.
E5
mf w/ dist.
Gtrs. 3 & 4
mf
P.M.

2.
4.
D.S.S. al Coda 2
*G5/E
E5
G5/E
E5 N.C.
fdbk.
Pitch: B
P.M.
*Bass plays E.
Coda 2
Gtrs. 3 & 4: w/ Rhy. Fig. 2
C5
G/B
A5
We are the un - der - rat - ed, all for - got - ten
F5
C5
G/B
kids who made it. Speak up now, lose or get
Outro
Gtr. 3: w/ Rhy. Fig. 1
A5
F5
C♯5
G♯5
E5
left be - hind.
Gtrs. 3 & 4

Watch the World

Words and Music by Tom De Longe and Travis Barker

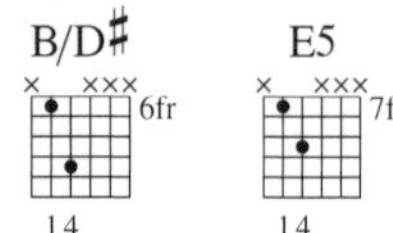

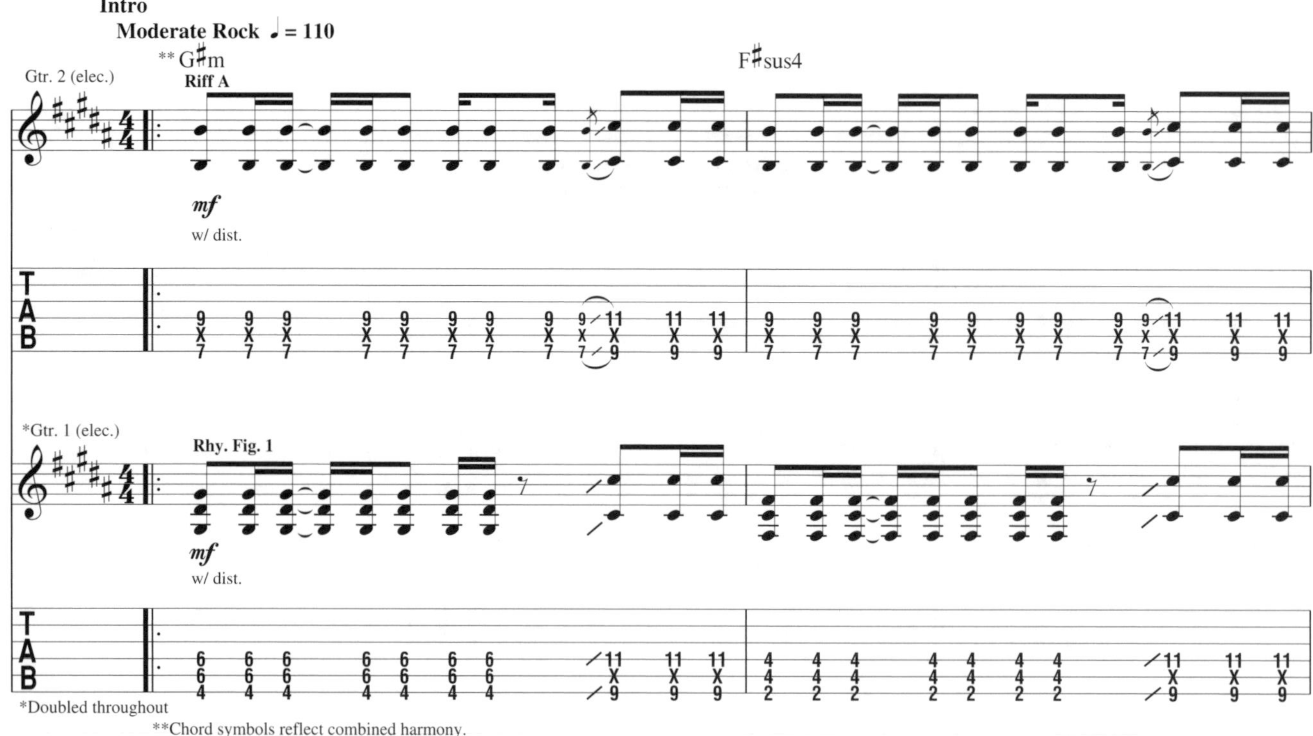

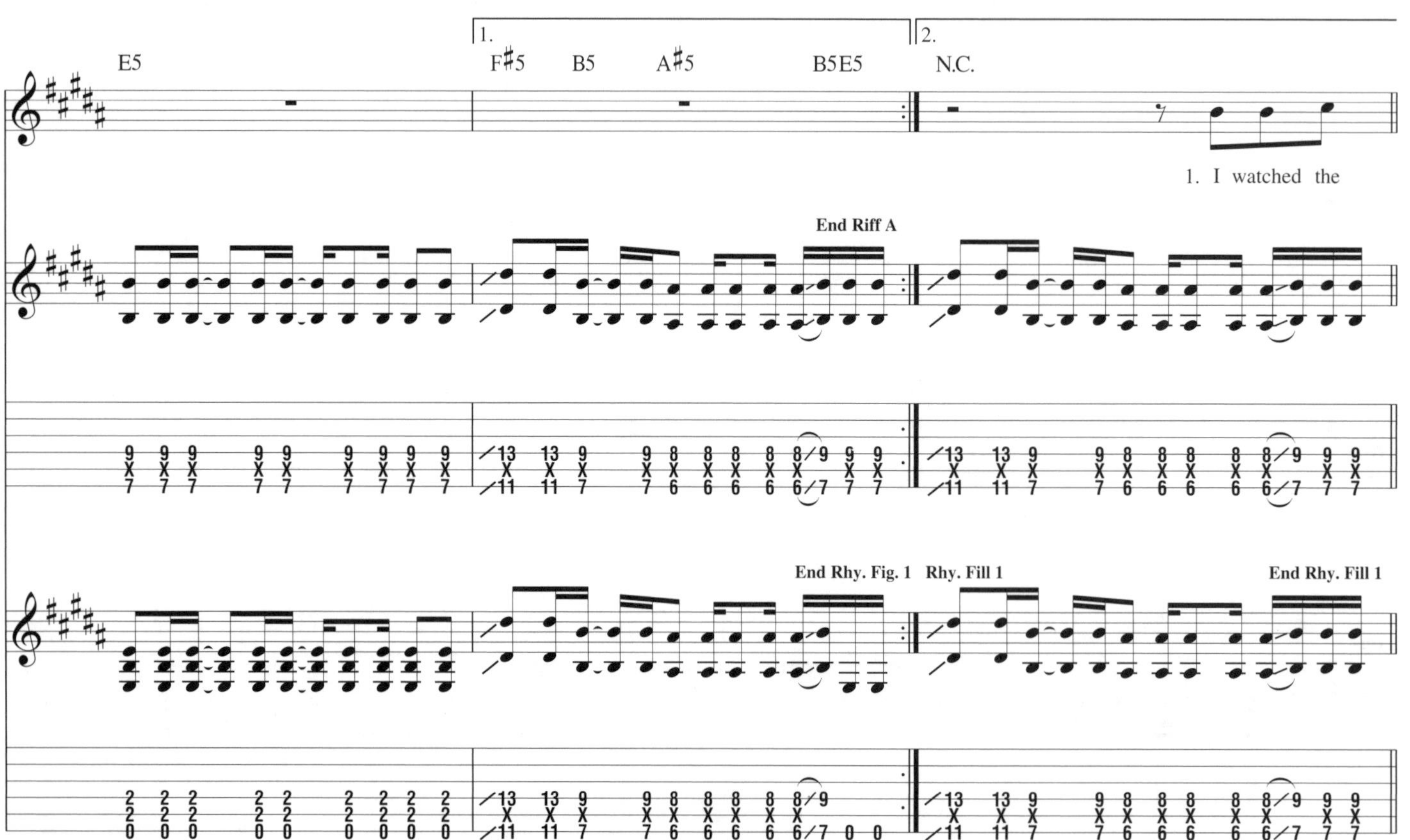

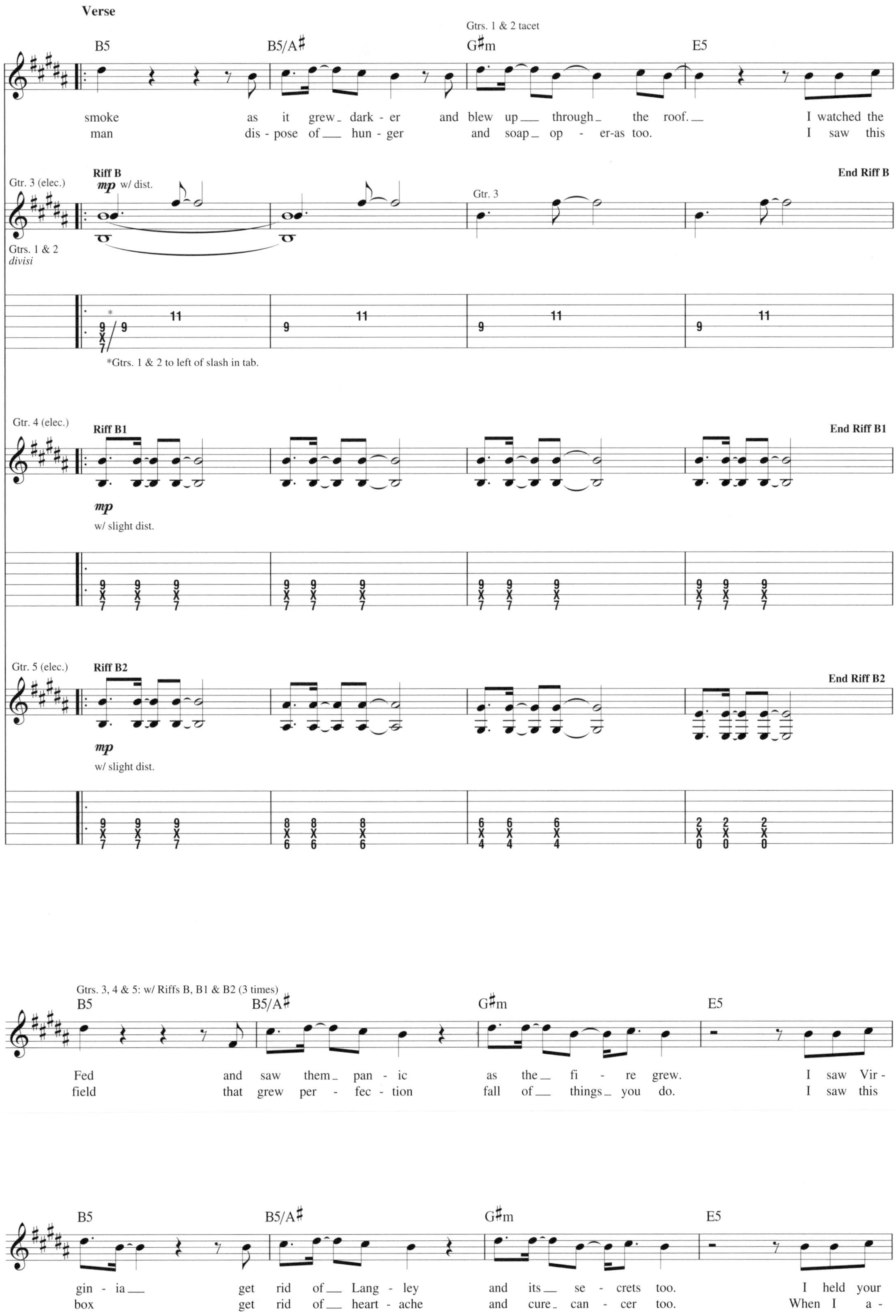

Verse

Gtrs. 1 & 2 tacet

B5 B5/A♯ G♯m E5

smoke as it grew dark - er and blew up through the roof. I watched the
man dis - pose of hun - ger and soap op - er-as too. I saw this

Gtr. 3 (elec.)
Riff B
mp w/ dist.
Gtr. 3
End Riff B
Gtrs. 1 & 2
divisi

*Gtrs. 1 & 2 to left of slash in tab.

Gtr. 4 (elec.)
Riff B1
End Riff B1
mp
w/ slight dist.

Gtr. 5 (elec.)
Riff B2
End Riff B2
mp
w/ slight dist.

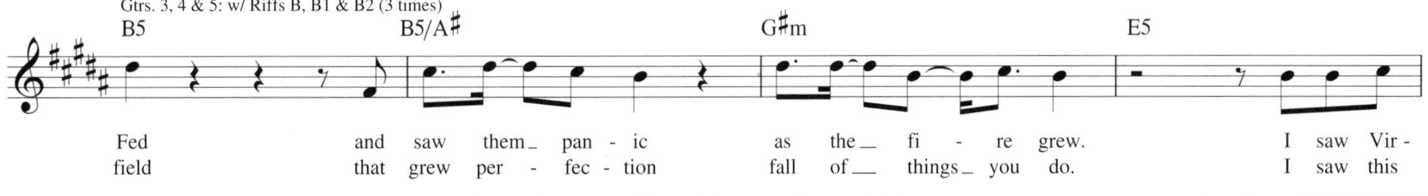

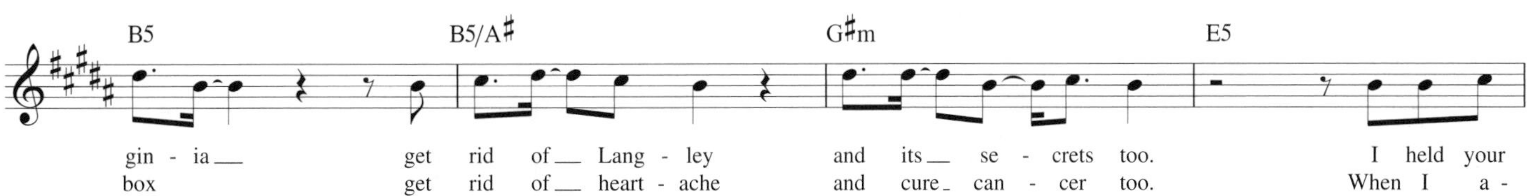

1.
B5
B5/A♯
G♯m
E5
hand and sat there_ know - ing that we'd_ make_ it through.
woke, I sat there_ hop - ing
Gtr. 2
*Vol. swell

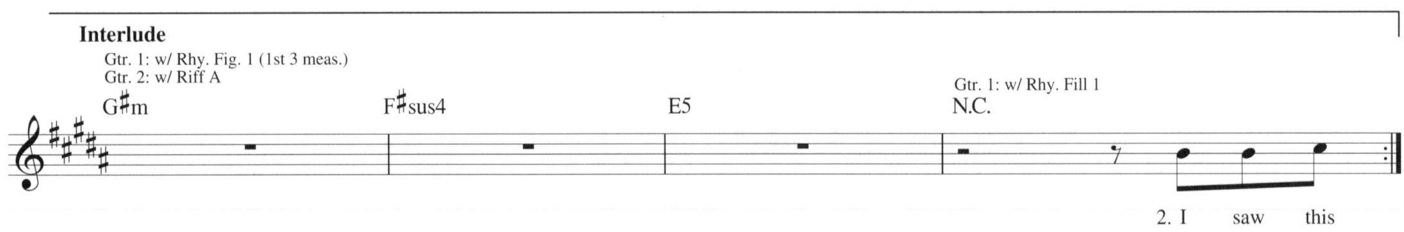

Interlude
Gtr. 1: w/ Rhy. Fig. 1 (1st 3 meas.)
Gtr. 2: w/ Riff A
G♯m
F♯sus4
E5
Gtr. 1: w/ Rhy. Fill 1
N.C.
2. I saw this

2.
Chorus
G♯m
E5
B5
this is___ what___ we'll do: If we can, we will
Gtr. 2
Riff C1
mp
fdbk.
f
Gtr. 1
Riff C
f

G♯m
F♯sus4
leave a let-ter and this song for you. And we'll
End Riff C1
End Riff C
1st time, Gtrs. 1 & 2: w/ Riffs C & C1 (2 times)
2nd time, Gtrs. 1 & 2: w/ Riffs C & C1 (3 times)
To Coda
B5
write once a day and put it through the sea to you. We'll re-
gret all those things we thought of but did-n't ev-er do.
Interlude
B/D♯
G♯5 D♯5
E5
Gtr. 2
Gtr. 1
Gtr. 1 tacet
1., 2., 3.
4.
D.S. al Coda
(cont. in notation)
If we
Gtr. 6 (acous.)
let ring

Coda
Gtr. 3: w/ Riff B (2 times)
B5
G♯m
F♯sus4
gret all those things we thought of but did - n't ev - er do. When the

B5
G♯m
F♯sus4
sky seems to clear, who will then be left but of you? Me and

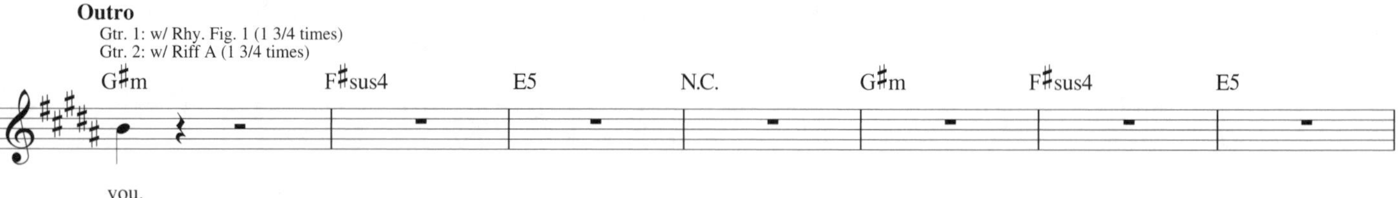
Outro
Gtr. 1: w/ Rhy. Fig. 1 (1 3/4 times)
Gtr. 2: w/ Riff A (1 3/4 times)
G♯m
F♯sus4
E5
N.C.
G♯m
F♯sus4
E5
you.

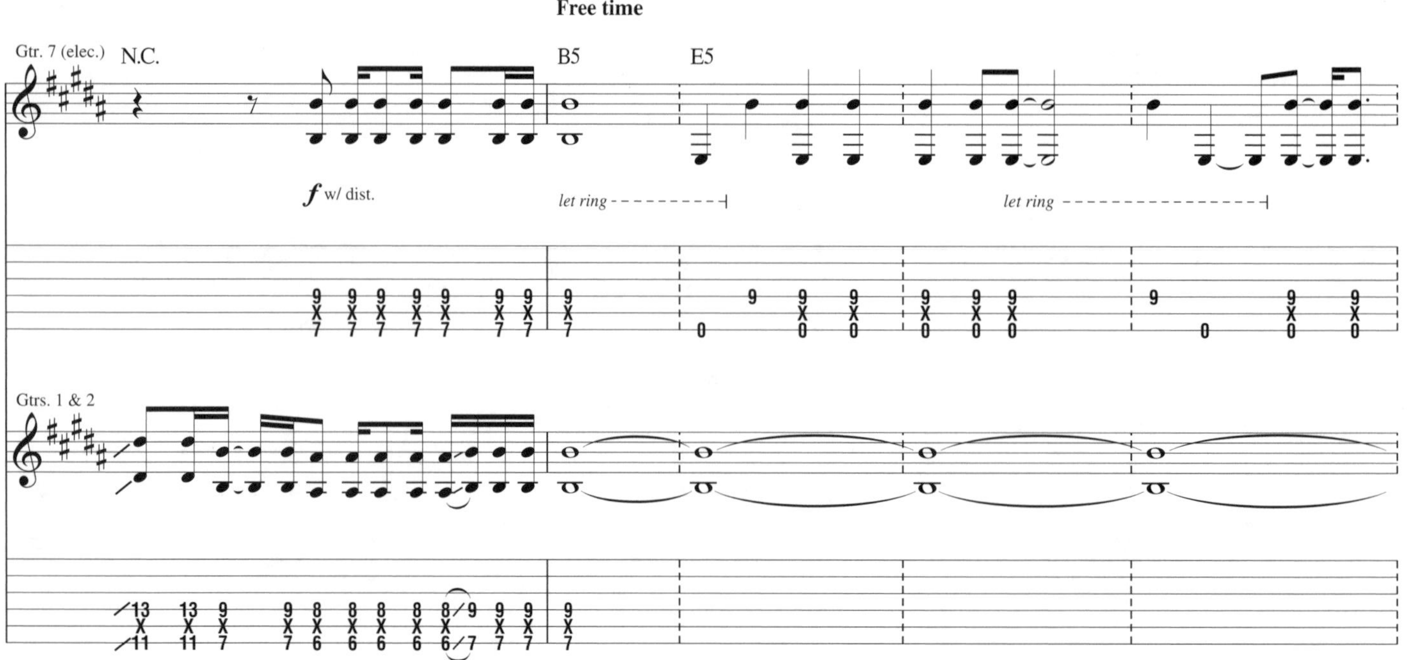
Free time
Gtr. 7 (elec.)
N.C.
B5
E5
f w/ dist.
let ring
let ring
Gtrs. 1 & 2

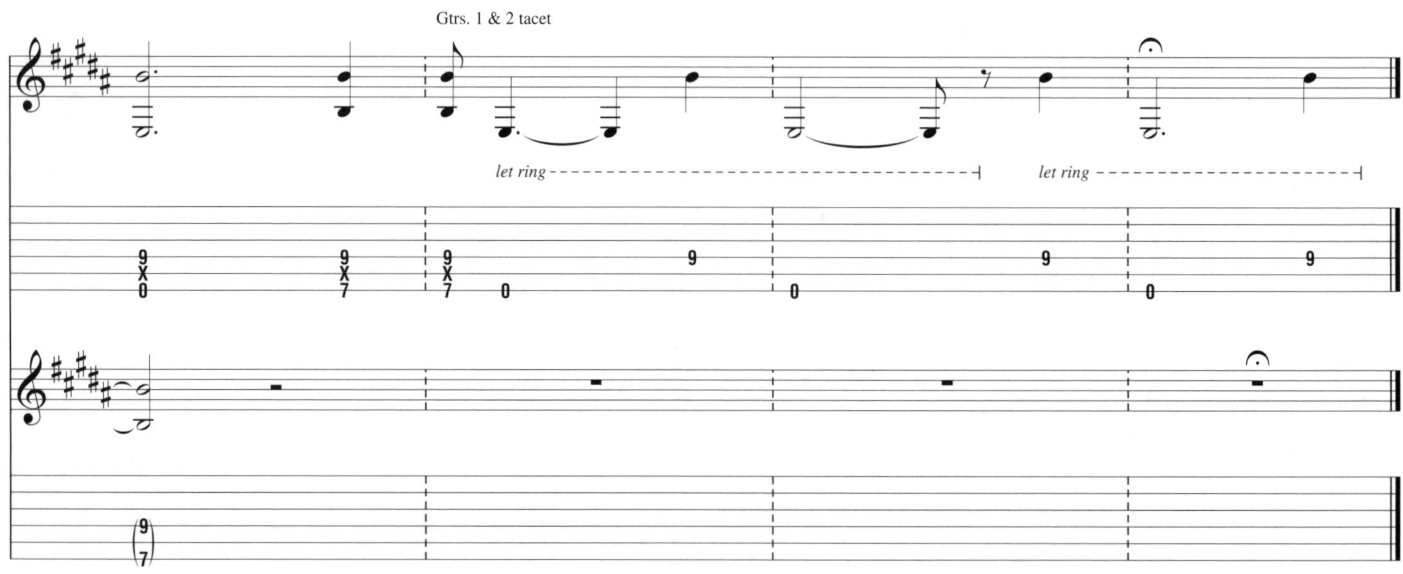
Gtrs. 1 & 2 tacet
let ring
let ring

Tiny Voices

Words and Music by Tom De Longe and Travis Barker

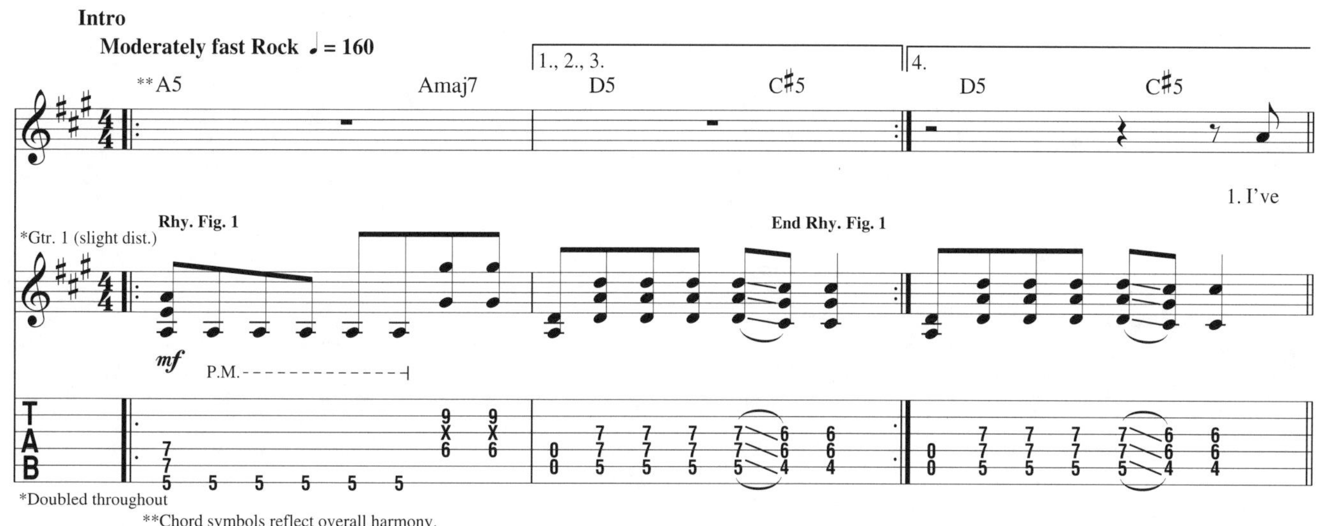

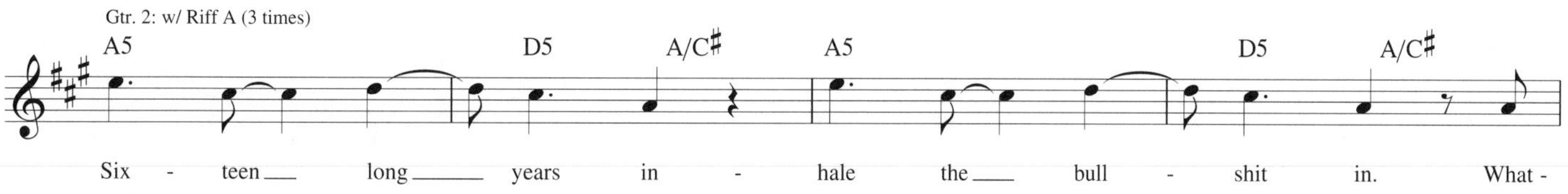

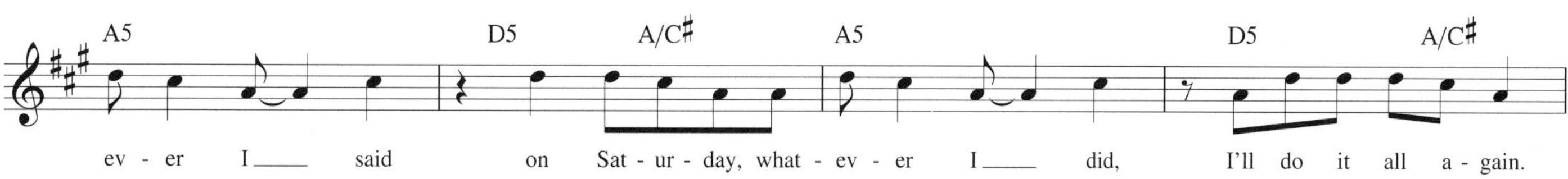

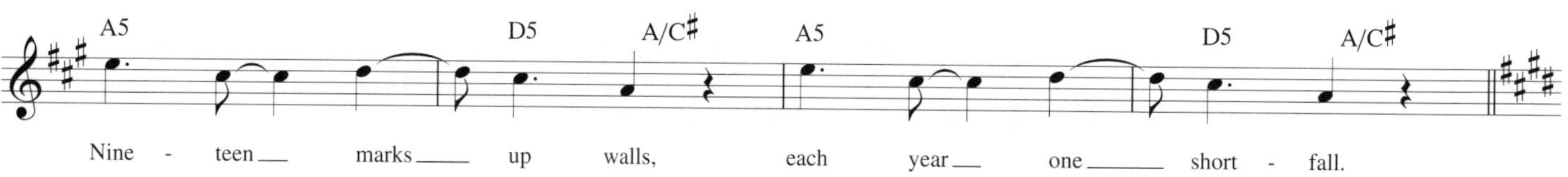
A5
D5
A/C♯
A5
D5
A/C♯
Nine - teen marks up walls, each year one short - fall.

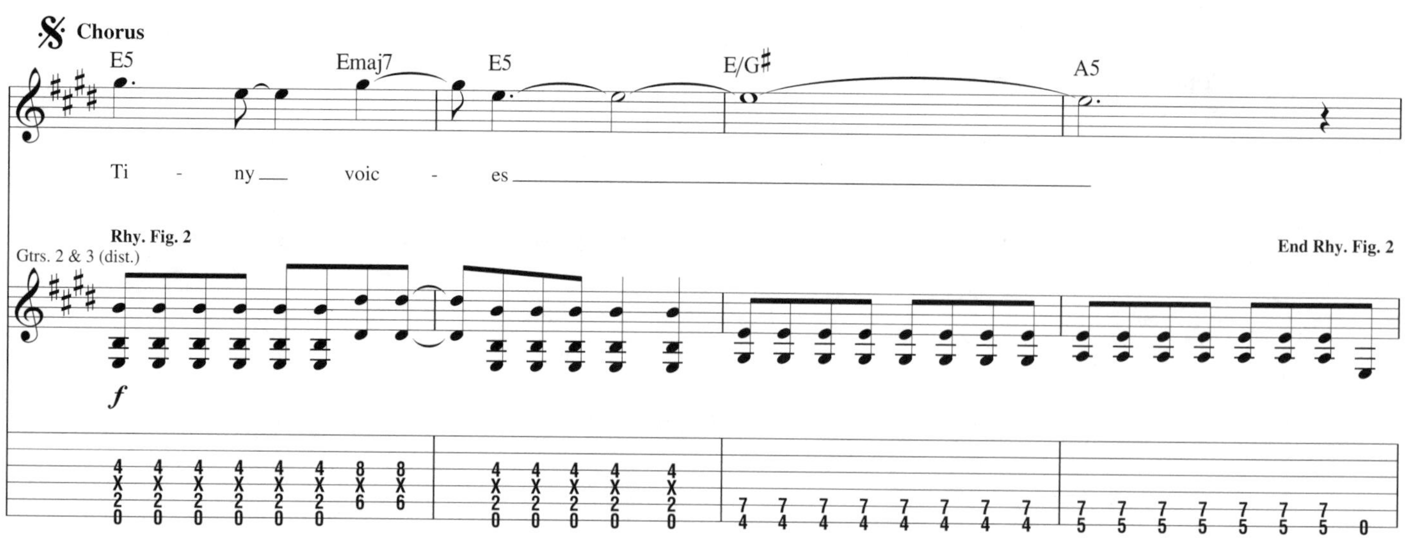
Chorus
E5
Emaj7
E5
E/G♯
A5
Ti - ny voic - es
Rhy. Fig. 2
Gtrs. 2 & 3 (dist.)
End Rhy. Fig. 2
f

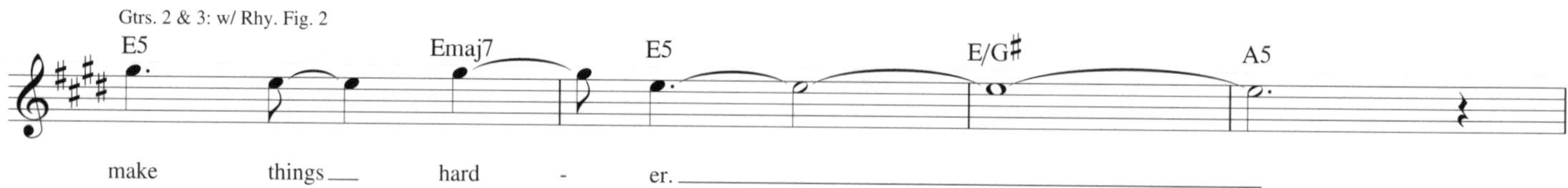
Gtrs. 2 & 3: w/ Rhy. Fig. 2
E5
Emaj7
E5
E/G♯
A5
make things hard - er.

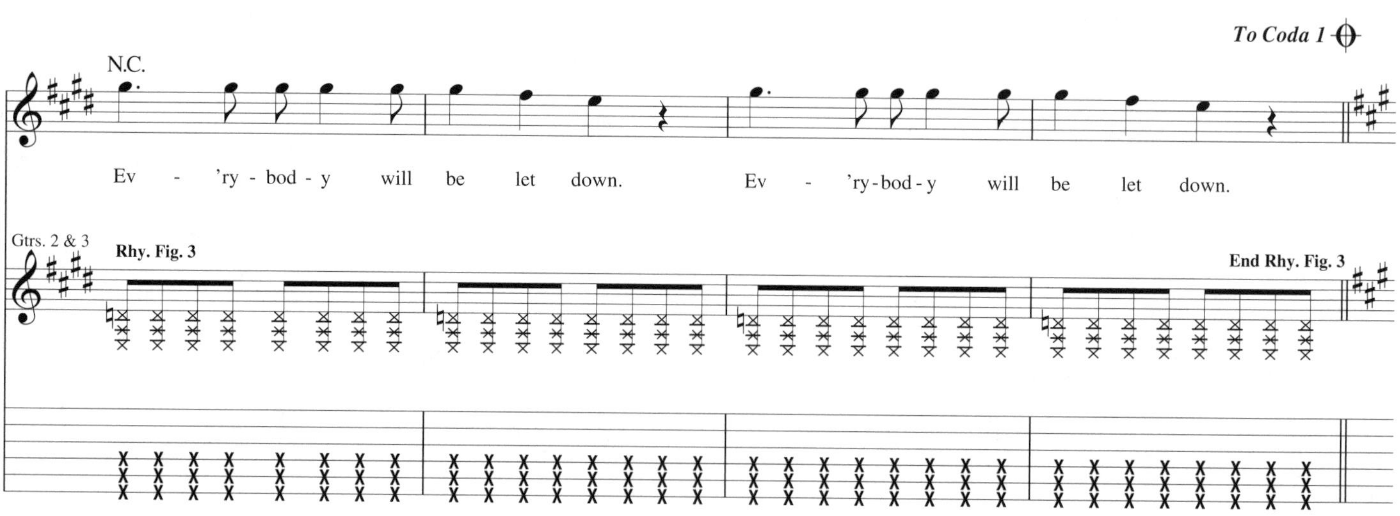
To Coda 1
N.C.
Ev - 'ry - bod - y will be let down. Ev - 'ry-bod - y will be let down.
Gtrs. 2 & 3
Rhy. Fig. 3
End Rhy. Fig. 3

Interlude

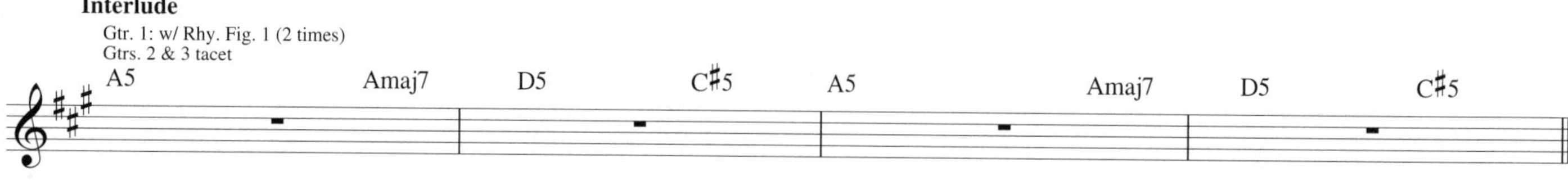
Gtr. 1: w/ Rhy. Fig. 1 (2 times)
Gtrs. 2 & 3 tacet
A5
Amaj7
D5
C♯5
A5
Amaj7
D5
C♯5

Verse
Gtr. 2: w/ Riff A (2 times)
A5
D5
A/C♯
A5
D5
A/C♯
2.What is this___ for? Ex - park - ing lot. The dream - ers go___ buy, they nev - er stop.

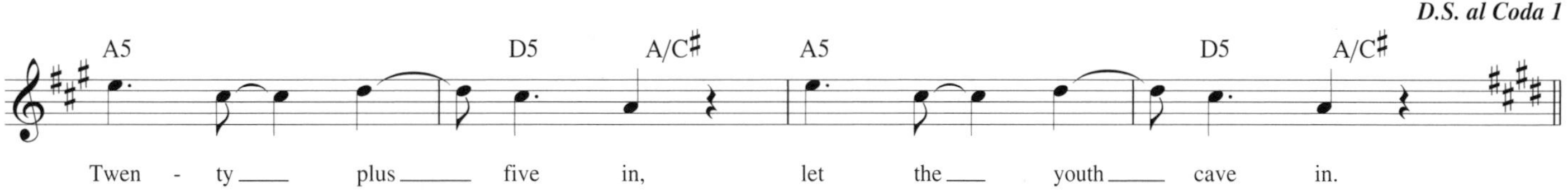
D.S. al Coda 1
A5
D5
A/C♯
A5
D5
A/C♯
Twen - ty___ plus___ five in, let the___ youth___ cave in.

Coda 1
Interlude
Gtrs. 2 & 3 tacet
E5
Esus2
Gtr. 5 (slight dist.)
mp
Riff B
Gtr. 4 (clean)
mp
let ring

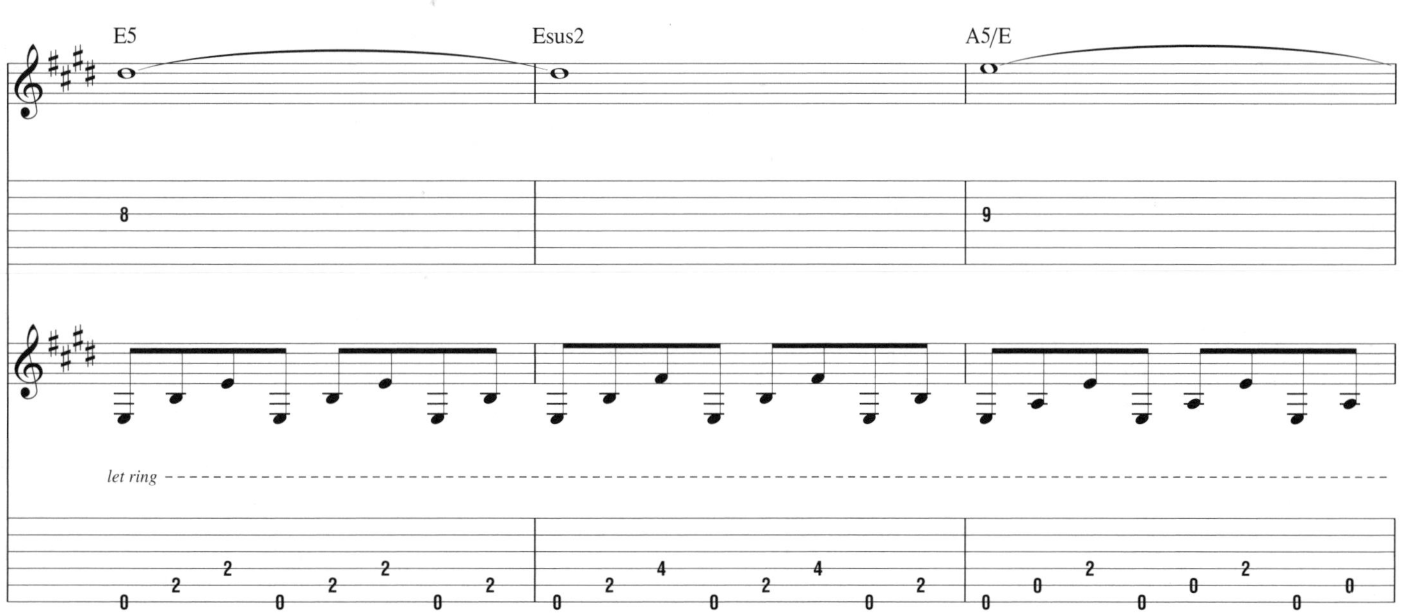
E5
Esus2
A5/E
let ring

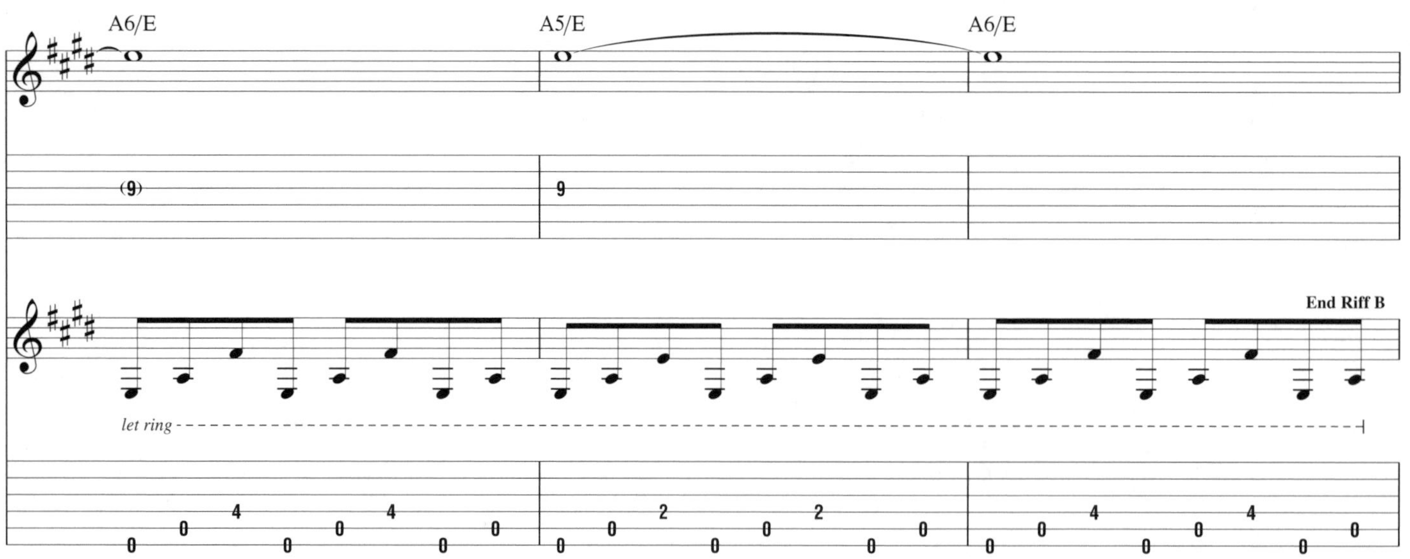

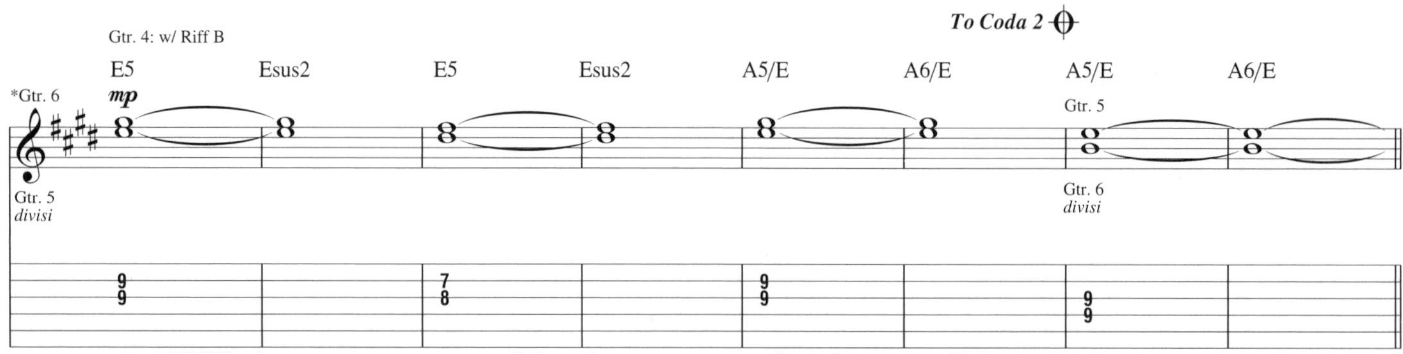

*Piano arr. for gtr.

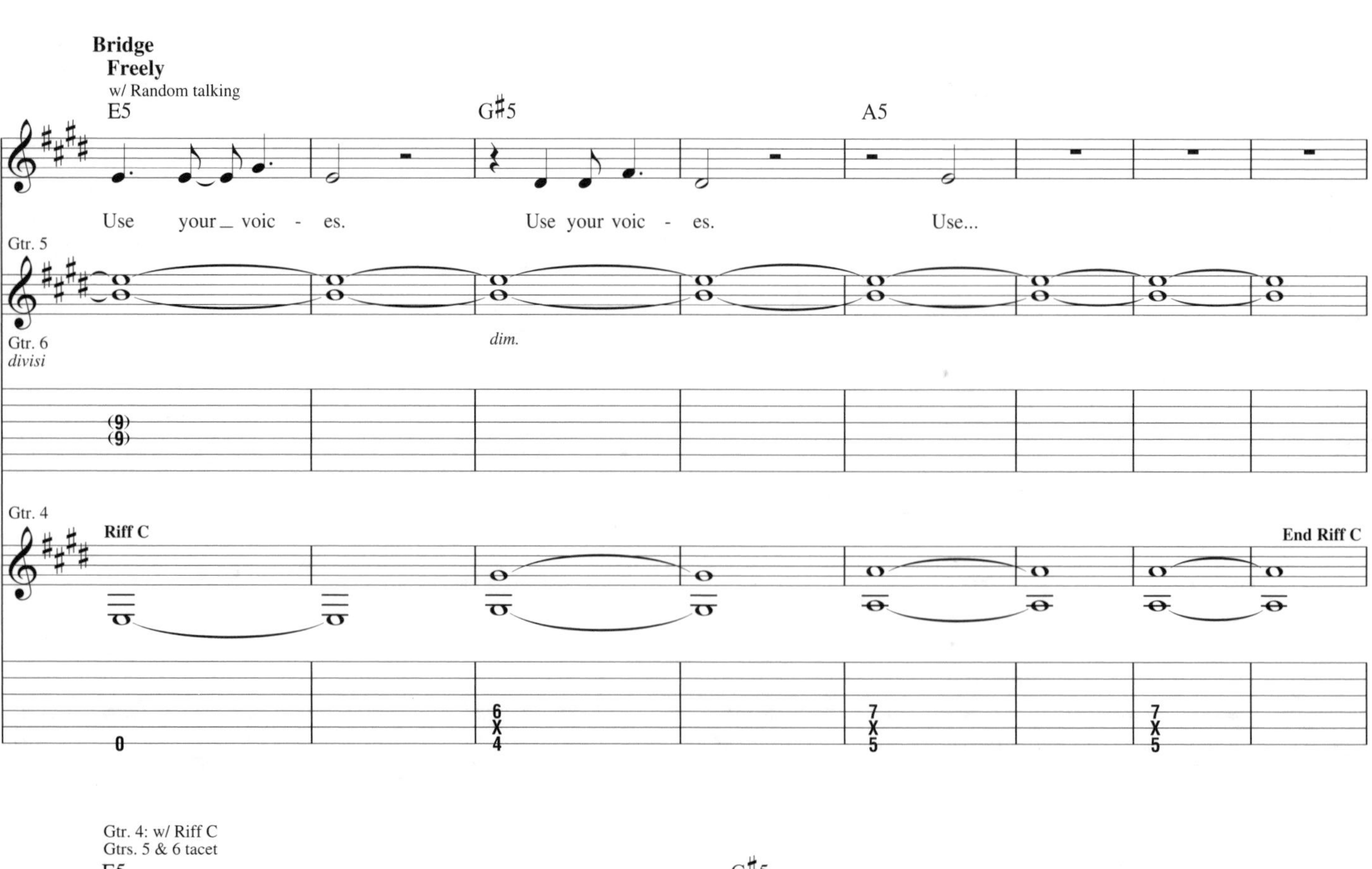

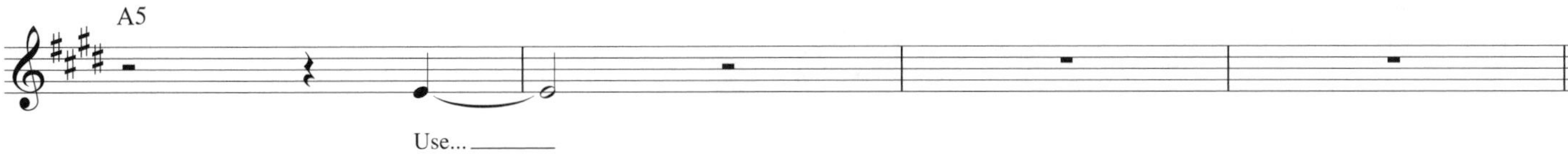
A5
Use...

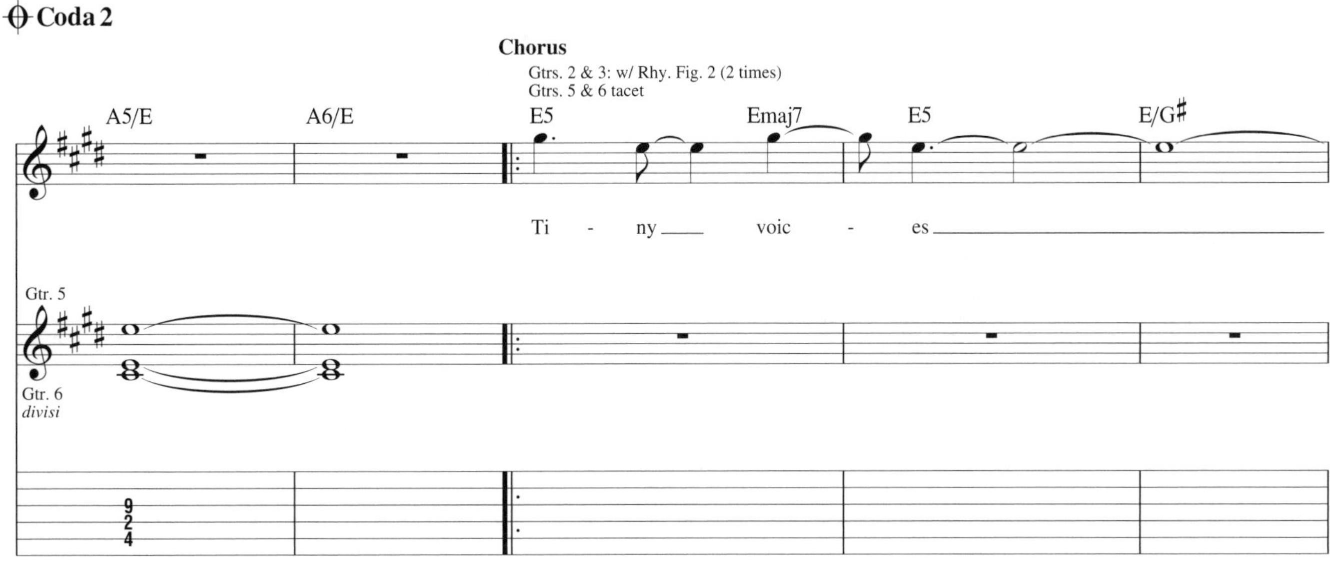
Coda 2
Chorus
Gtrs. 2 & 3: w/ Rhy. Fig. 2 (2 times)
Gtrs. 5 & 6 tacet
A5/E
A6/E
E5
Emaj7
E5
E/G♯
Ti - ny voic - es
Gtr. 5
Gtr. 6
divisi
9
2
4

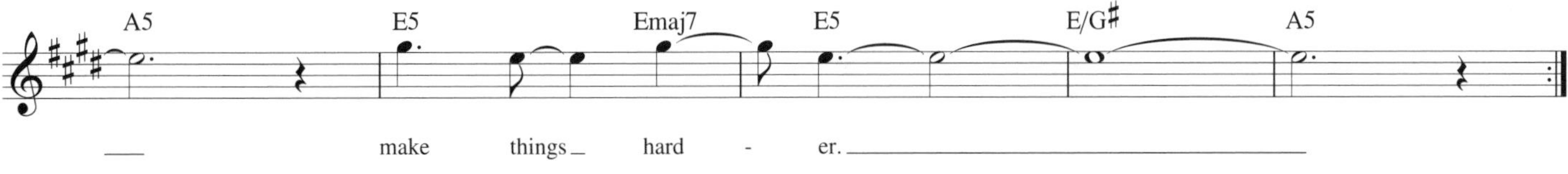
A5
E5
Emaj7
E5
E/G♯
A5
make things hard - er.

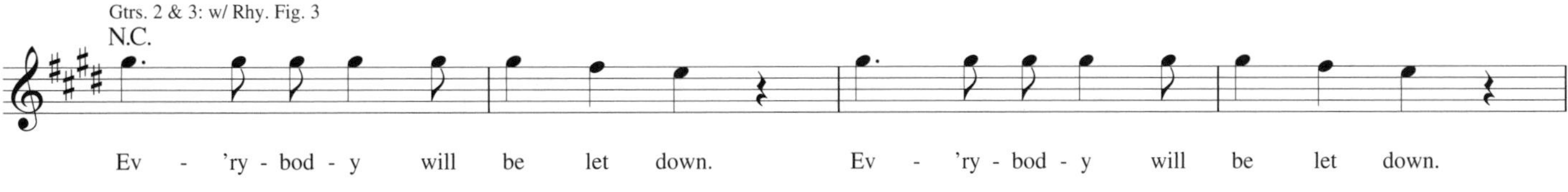
Gtrs. 2 & 3: w/ Rhy. Fig. 3
N.C.
Ev - 'ry - bod - y will be let down. Ev - 'ry - bod - y will be let down.

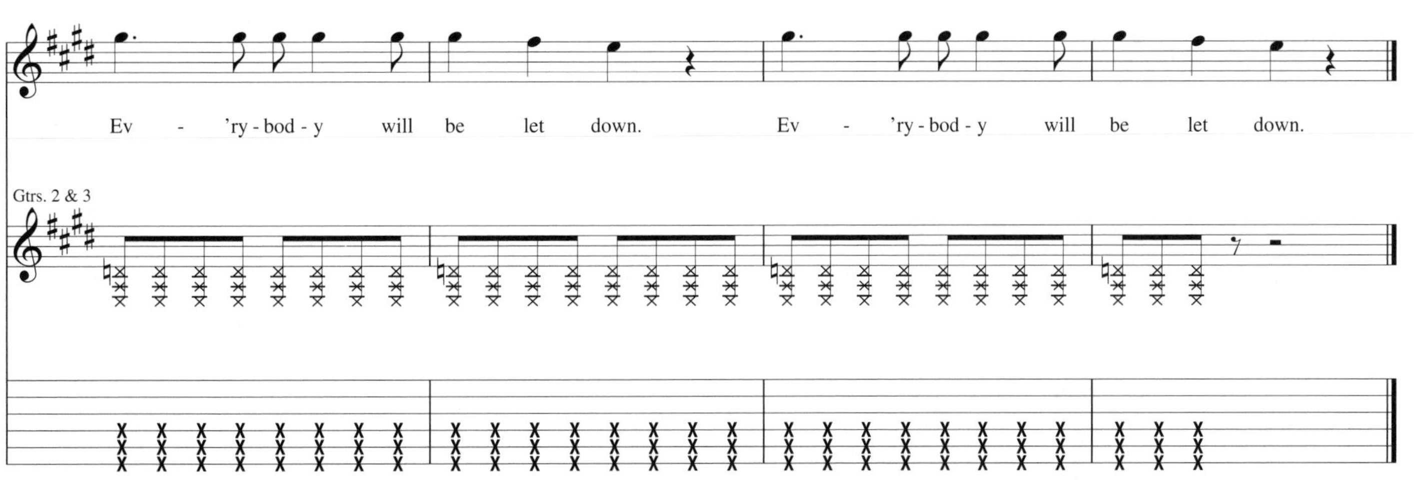
Ev - 'ry - bod - y will be let down. Ev - 'ry - bod - y will be let down.
Gtrs. 2 & 3

Cat Like Thief

Words and Music by Tom De Longe, Travis Barker and Tim Armstrong

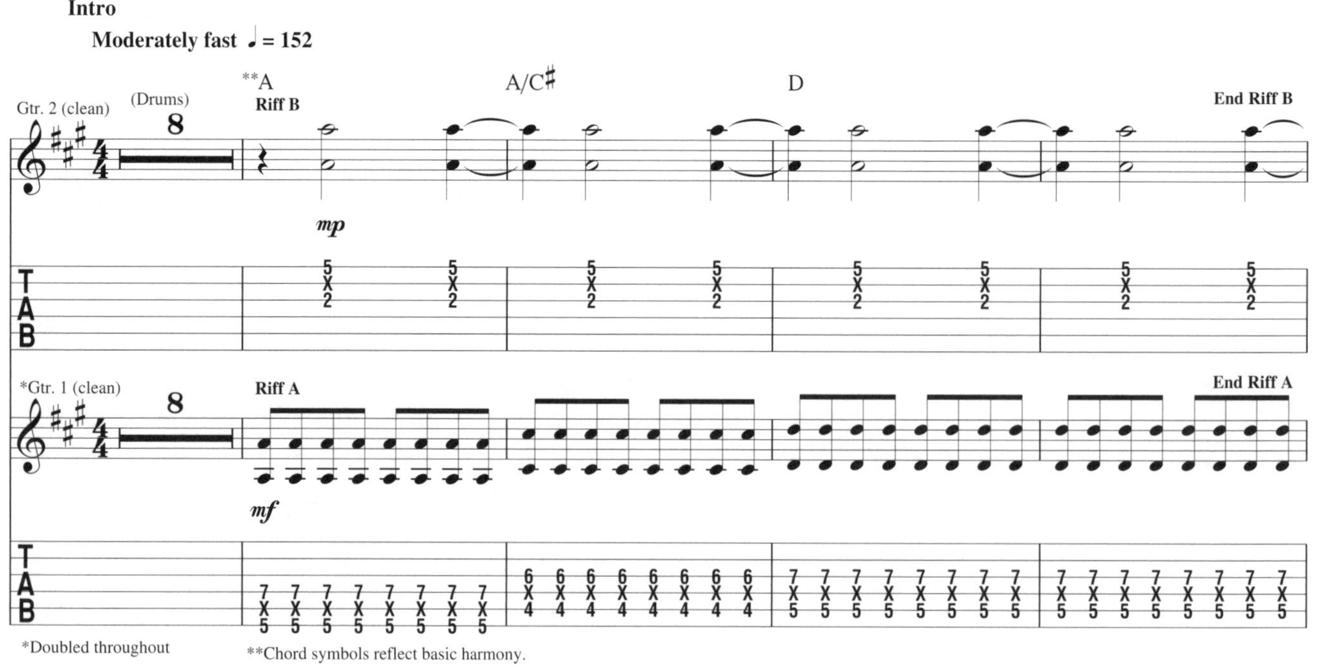

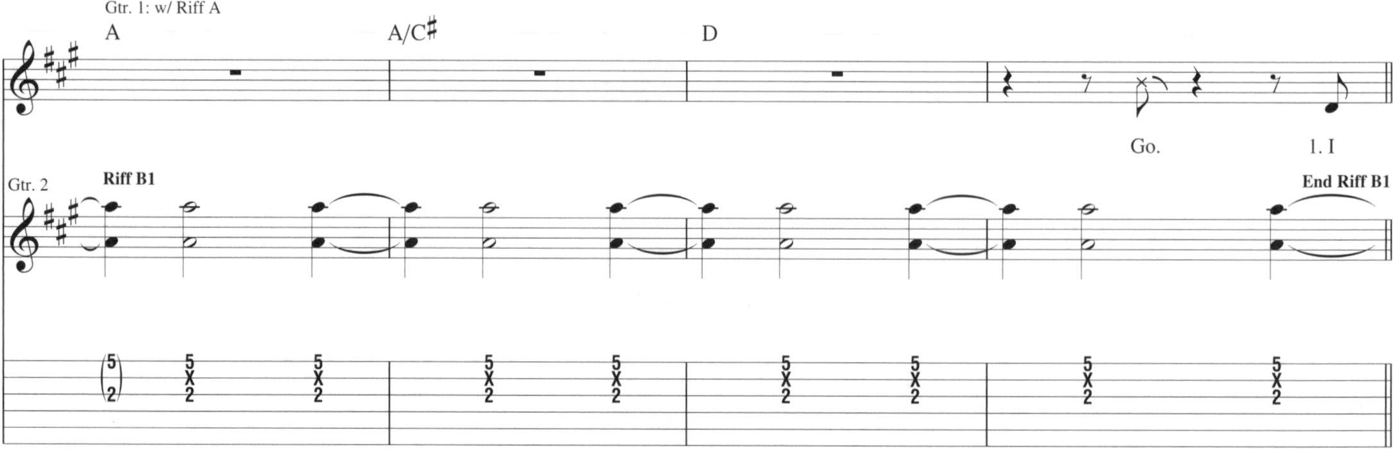

Pre-Chorus

Gtrs. 1 & 2: w/ Riffs A & B1 (4 times)

A A/C♯ D

wrote it down, a list a month a - go.
Call me back when word is that she's gone.

A A/C♯ D

Six - teen chap - ters of one thing you've blown. The
Cat - like thief, she stole air from my lungs.

A A/C♯ D

best thing yet to help you through and through.
Leave me stand - ing on this lone - ly grave. I

A D *To Coda 2*

That she was, I feel her more than you.
dug it out in case she turns a - way.

Chorus

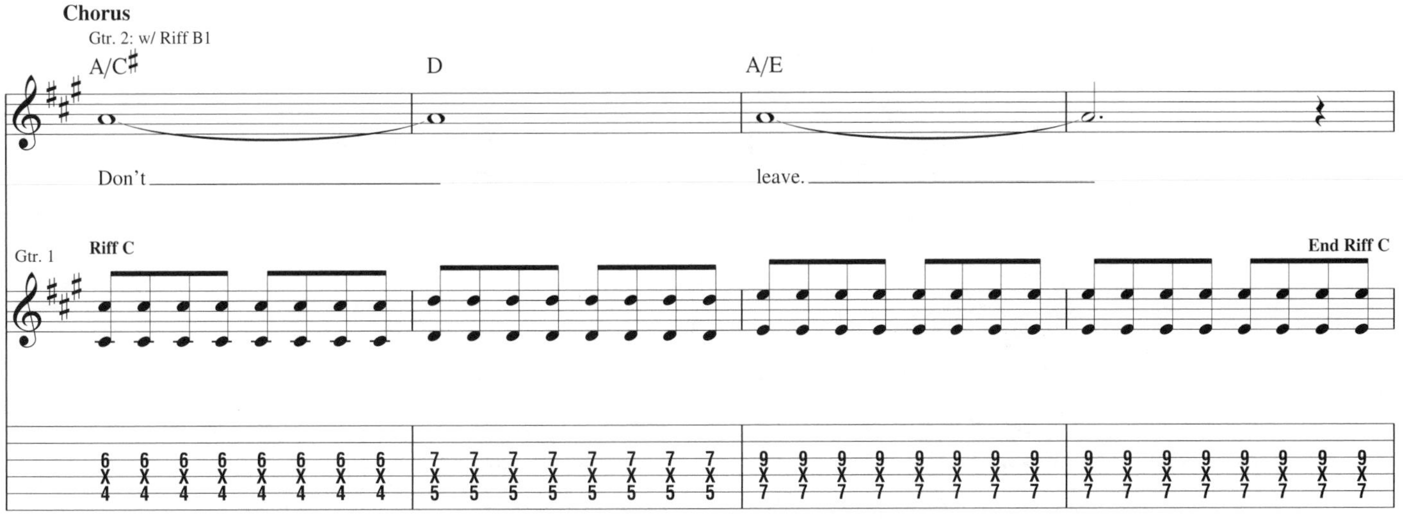

Gtr. 1 : w/ Riff C
A/C♯
D
A/E
E
Don't
leave
her.
Gtr. 2
Riff D
End Riff D
Interlude
Gtr. 1: w/ Riff A (2 times)
Gtr. 2: w/ Riff B
A
A/C♯
D
Gtr. 2: w/ Riff B1
D.S. al Coda
Yeah.
2. I
Coda 1
Gtrs. 1 & 2: w/ Riffs A & B1 (2 times)
You think you see me here all a - lone. Got my crew com - in' now one by one,
D.S.S. al Coda 2
two by two, three by three, four by four. Let's do some more.
Coda 2
Outro-Chorus
Gtr. 1: w/ Riff C (2 times)
1st time, Gtr. 2: w/ Riff B1
2nd time, Gtr. 2: w/ Riff B
Don't
leave.
Don't leave her, don't leave her, don't leave her.
Don't leave her, don't leave her, don't leave her.
Gtr. 2: w/ Riff D
Don't
leave
her.
Don't leave her, don't leave her, don't leave her.
Don't leave her, don't leave her, don't leave her.

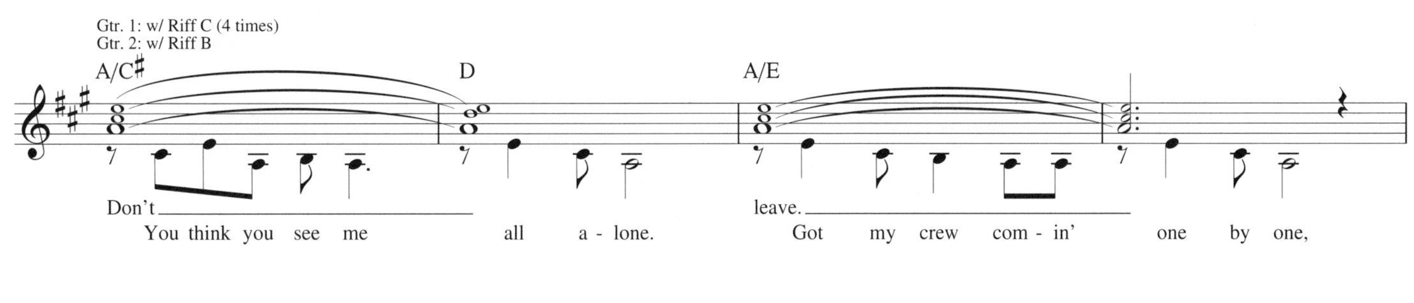
Gtr. 1: w/ Riff C (4 times)
Gtr. 2: w/ Riff B
A/C♯
D
A/E
Don't
leave.
You think you see me all a - lone.
Got my crew com - in' one by one,

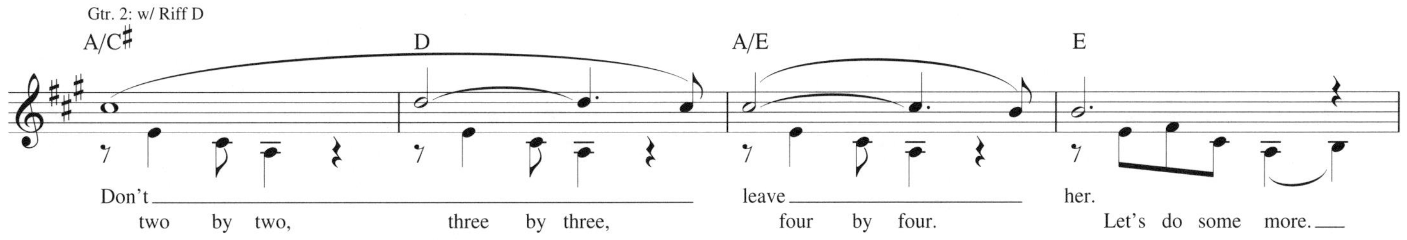
Gtr. 2: w/ Riff D
A/C♯
D
A/E
E
Don't
leave
her.
two by two, three by three,
four by four.
Let's do some more.

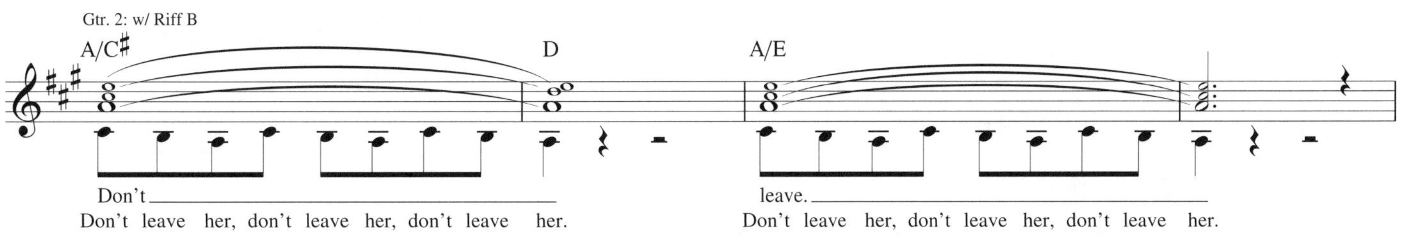
Gtr. 2: w/ Riff B
A/C♯
D
A/E
Don't
leave.
Don't leave her, don't leave her, don't leave her.
Don't leave her, don't leave her, don't leave her.

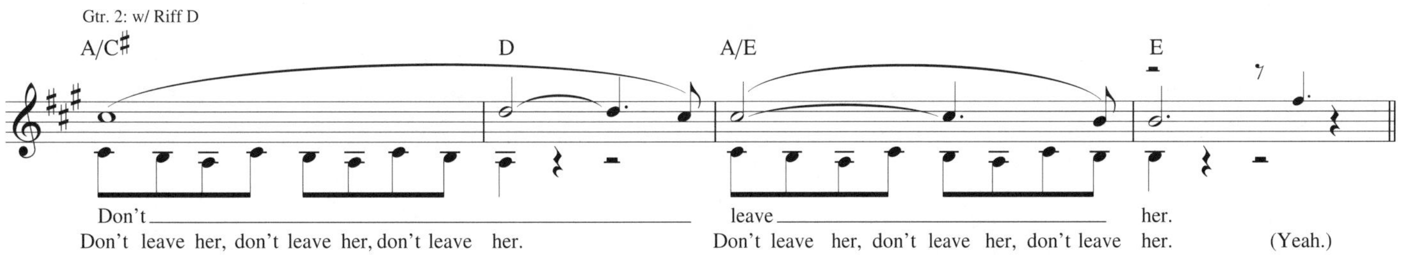
Gtr. 2: w/ Riff D
A/C♯
D
A/E
E
Don't
leave
her.
Don't leave her, don't leave her, don't leave her.
Don't leave her, don't leave her, don't leave her.
(Yeah.)

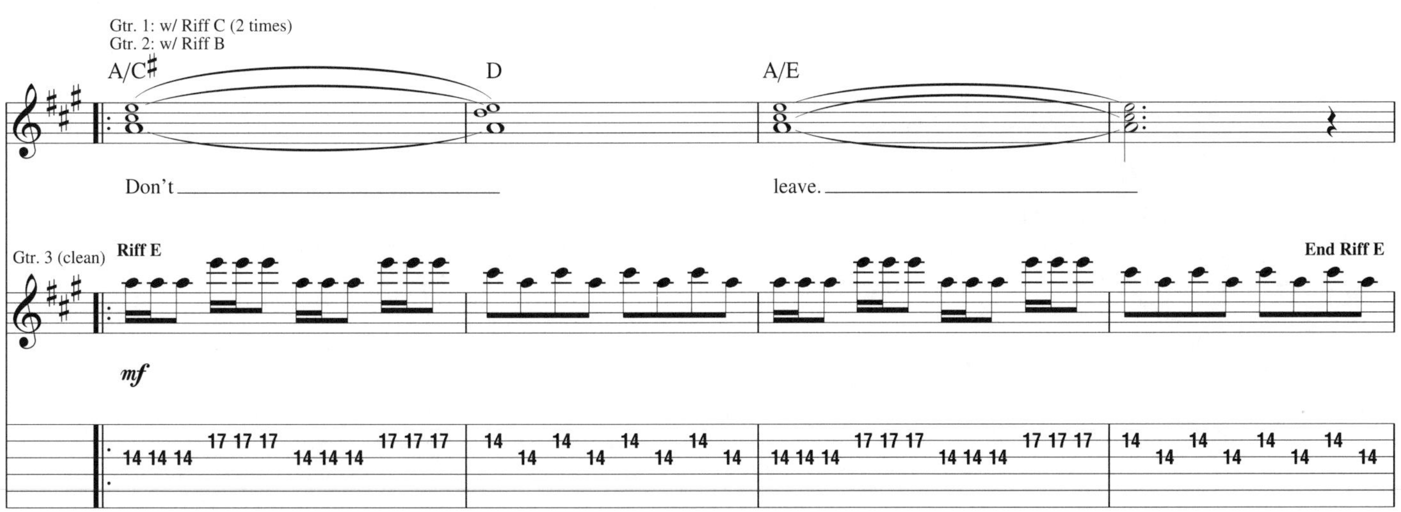
Gtr. 1: w/ Riff C (2 times)
Gtr. 2: w/ Riff B
A/C♯
D
A/E
Don't
leave.
Gtr. 3 (clean)
Riff E
End Riff E
mf

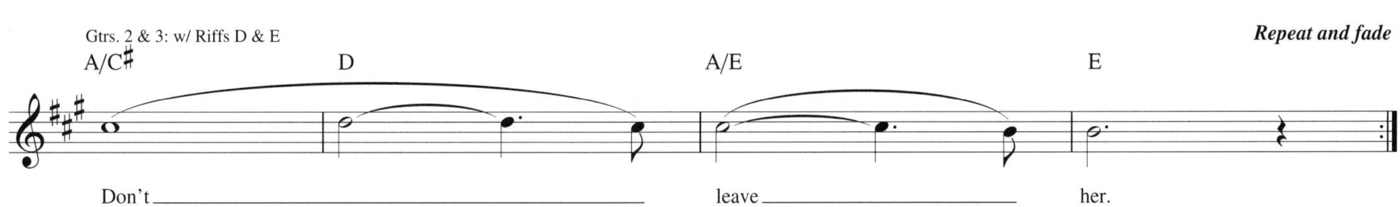
Gtrs. 2 & 3: w/ Riffs D & E
Repeat and fade
A/C♯
D
A/E
E
Don't
leave
her.

And I

Words and Music by Tom De Longe and Travis Barker

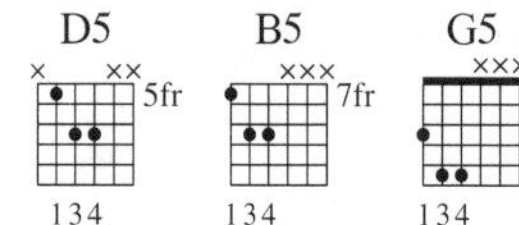

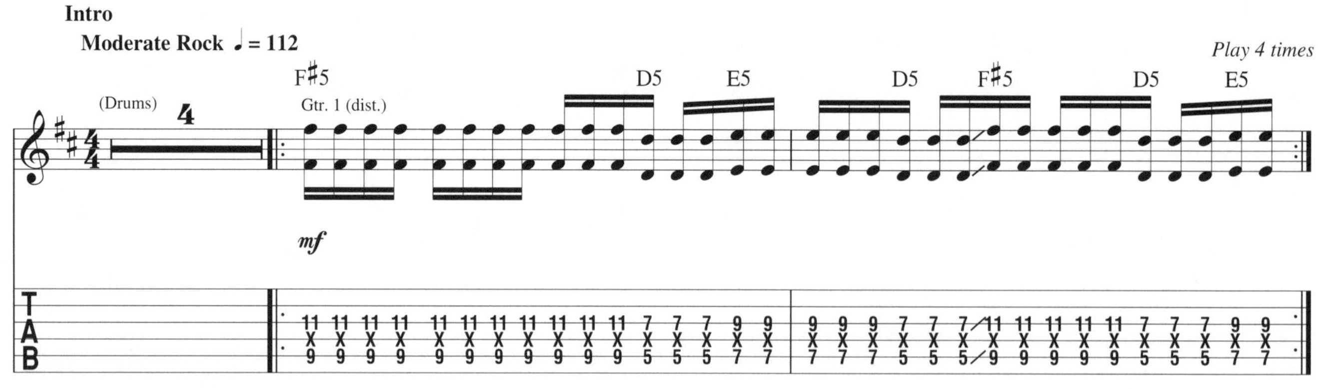

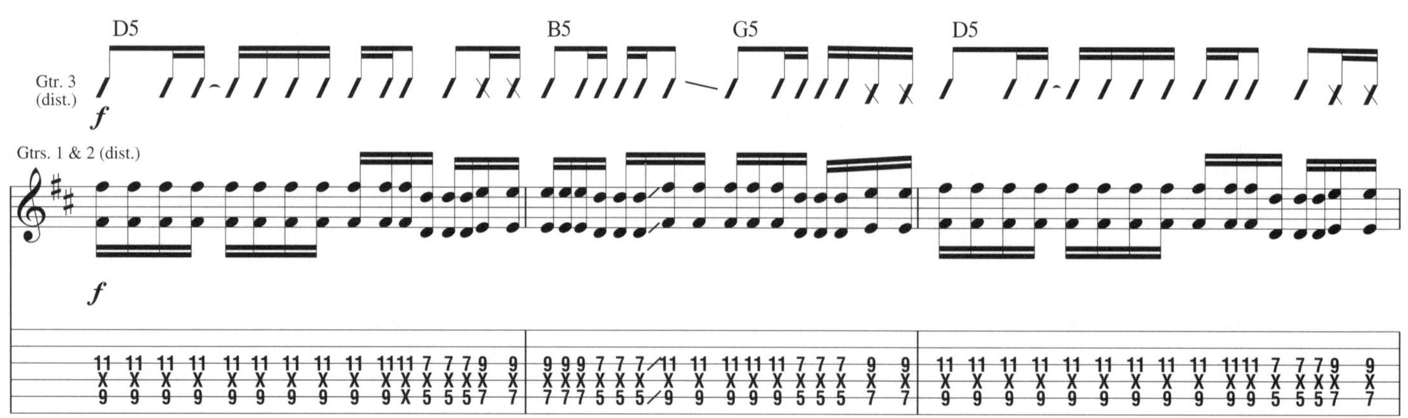

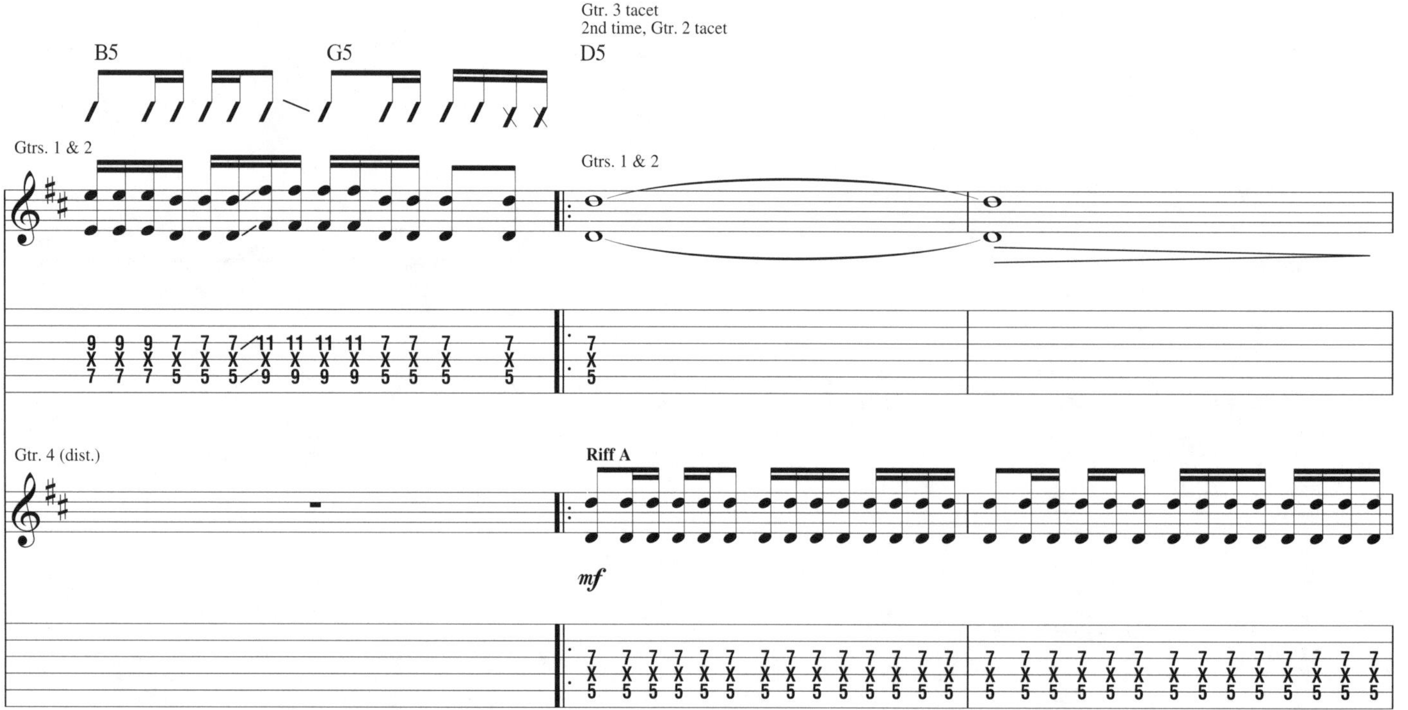

Gtrs. 1 & 2 tacet
Gtr. 4
End Riff A

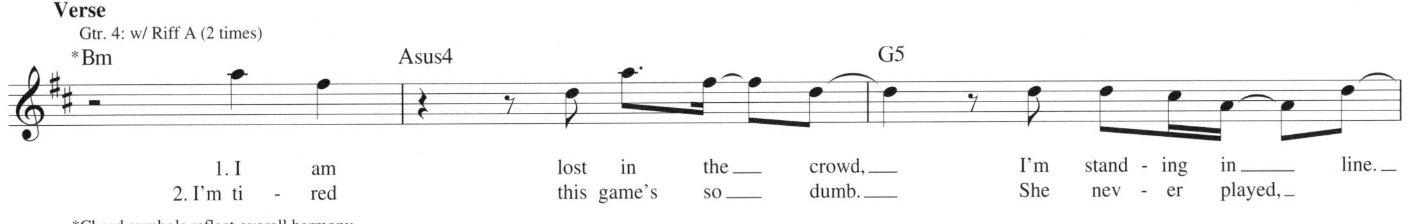
Verse
Gtr. 4: w/ Riff A (2 times)
*Bm
Asus4
G5
1. I am lost in the crowd, I'm stand - ing in line.
2. I'm ti - red this game's so dumb. She nev - er played,
*Chord symbols reflect overall harmony.

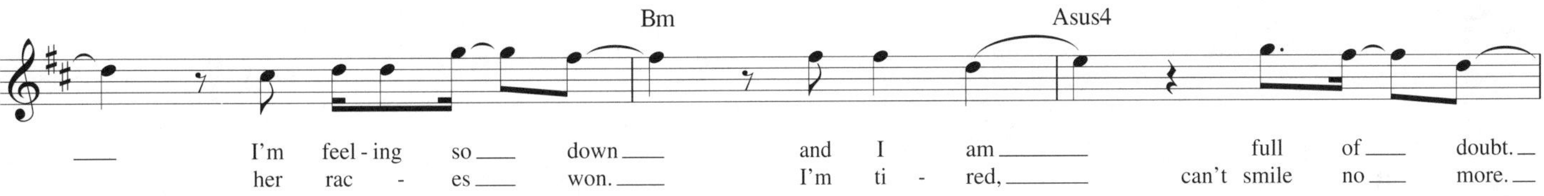
Bm
Asus4
I'm feel - ing so down and I am full of doubt.
her rac - es won. I'm ti - red, can't smile no more.

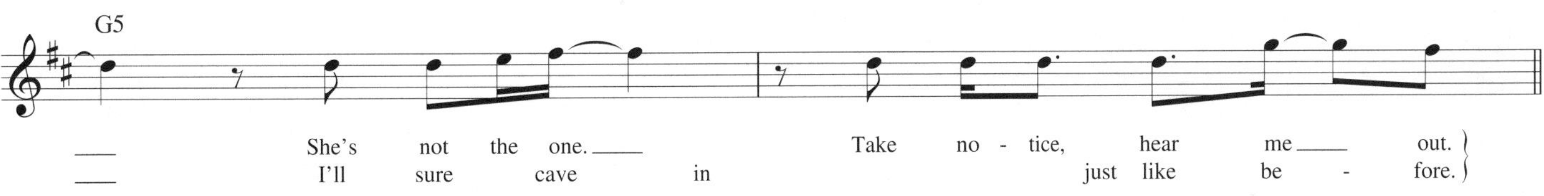
G5
She's not the one. Take no - tice, hear me out.
I'll sure cave in just like be - fore.

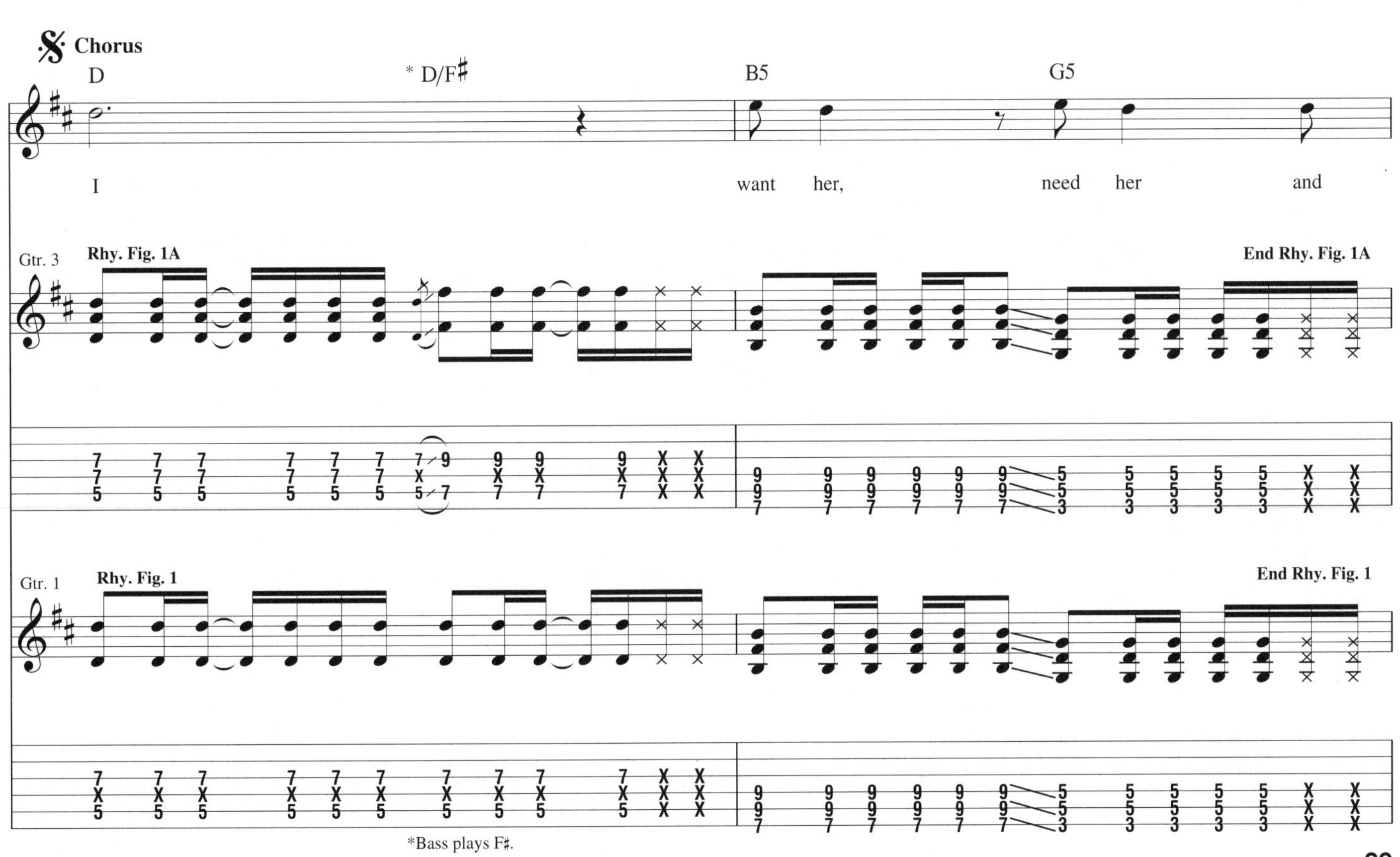
Chorus
D
*D/F♯
B5
G5
I want her, need her and
Gtr. 3
Rhy. Fig. 1A
End Rhy. Fig. 1A
Gtr. 1
Rhy. Fig. 1
End Rhy. Fig. 1
*Bass plays F♯.

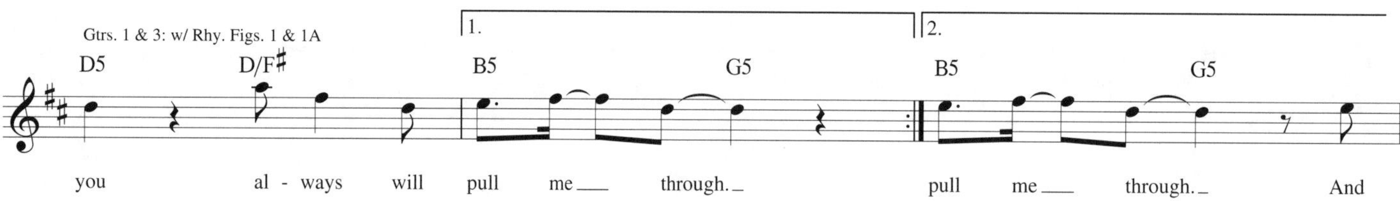
Gtrs. 1 & 3: w/ Rhy. Figs. 1 & 1A
1.
2.
D5
D/F♯
B5
G5
B5
G5
you al - ways will pull me through.
pull me through. And

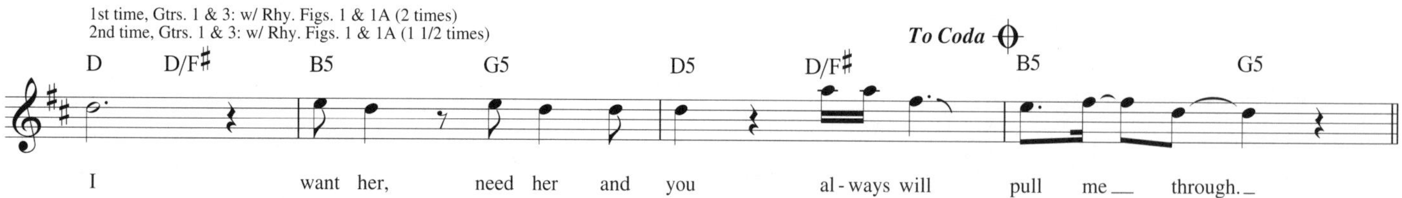
1st time, Gtrs. 1 & 3: w/ Rhy. Figs. 1 & 1A (2 times)
2nd time, Gtrs. 1 & 3: w/ Rhy. Figs. 1 & 1A (1 1/2 times)
To Coda
D
D/F♯
B5
G5
D5
D/F♯
B5
G5
I want her, need her and you al - ways will pull me through.

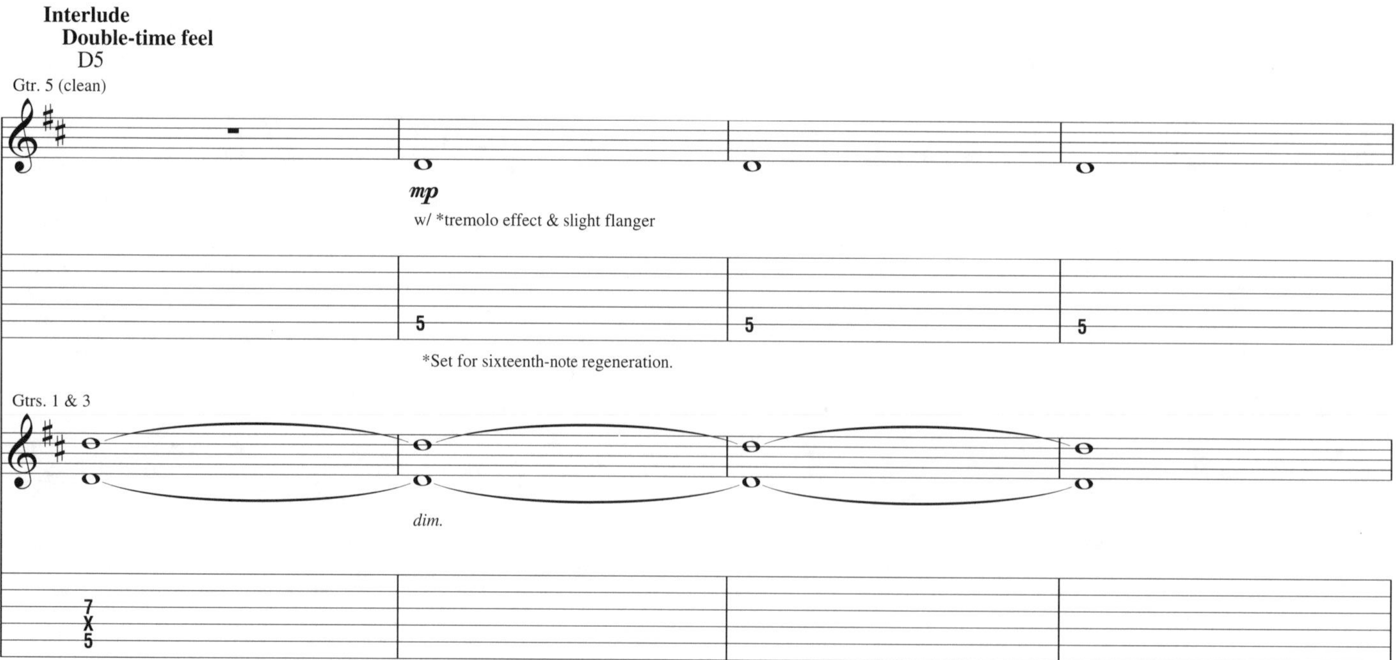
Interlude
Double-time feel
D5
Gtr. 5 (clean)
mp
w/ *tremolo effect & slight flanger
*Set for sixteenth-note regeneration.
Gtrs. 1 & 3
dim.

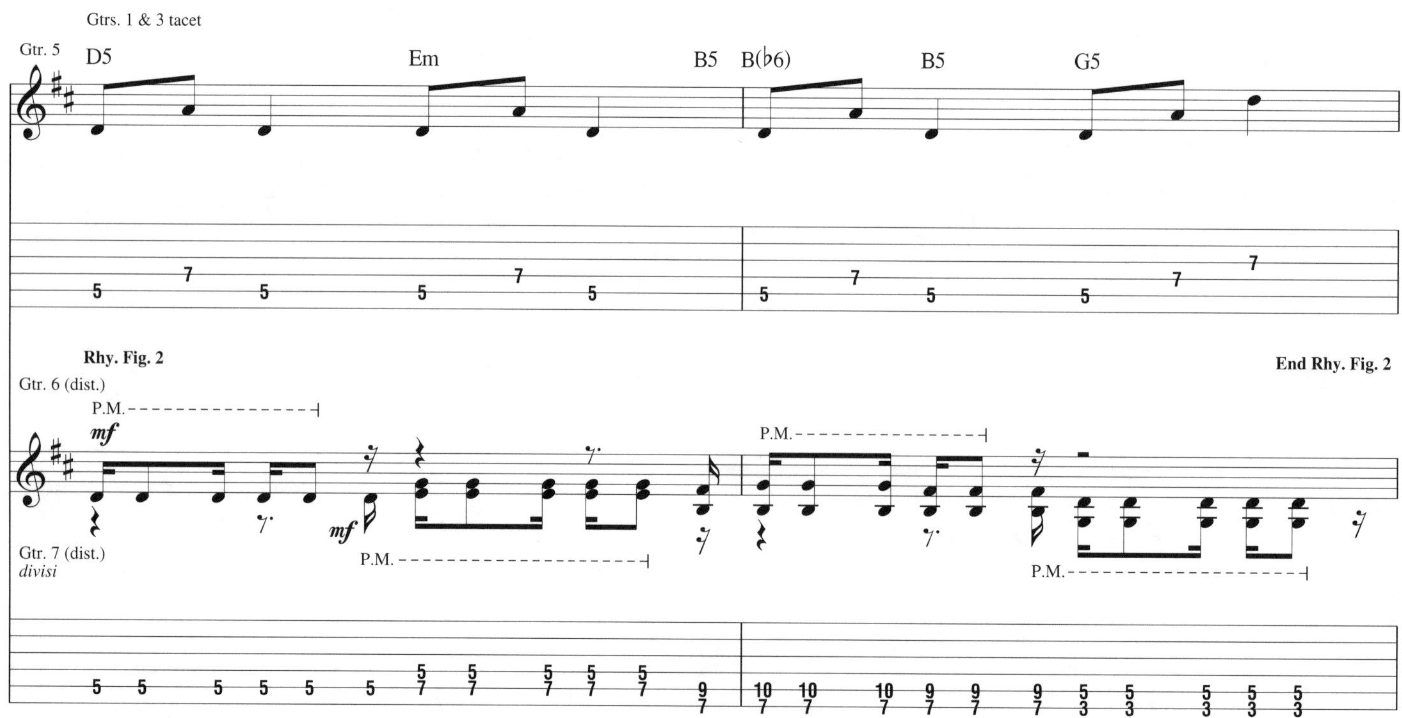
Gtrs. 1 & 3 tacet
Gtr. 5
D5
Em
B5
B(♭6)
B5
G5
Rhy. Fig. 2
End Rhy. Fig. 2
Gtr. 6 (dist.)
P.M.
mf
Gtr. 7 (dist.)
divisi

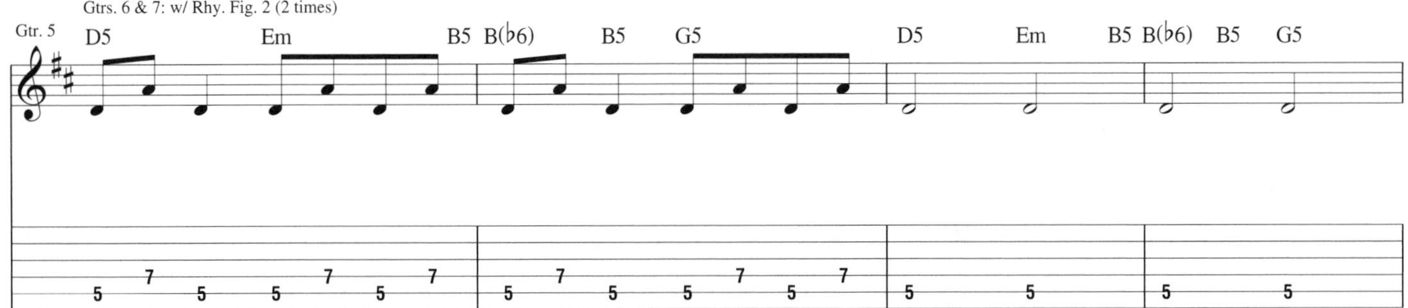
Gtrs. 6 & 7: w/ Rhy. Fig. 2 (2 times)
Gtr. 5
D5
Em
B5 B(♭6)
B5
G5
D5
Em
B5 B(♭6)
B5
G5

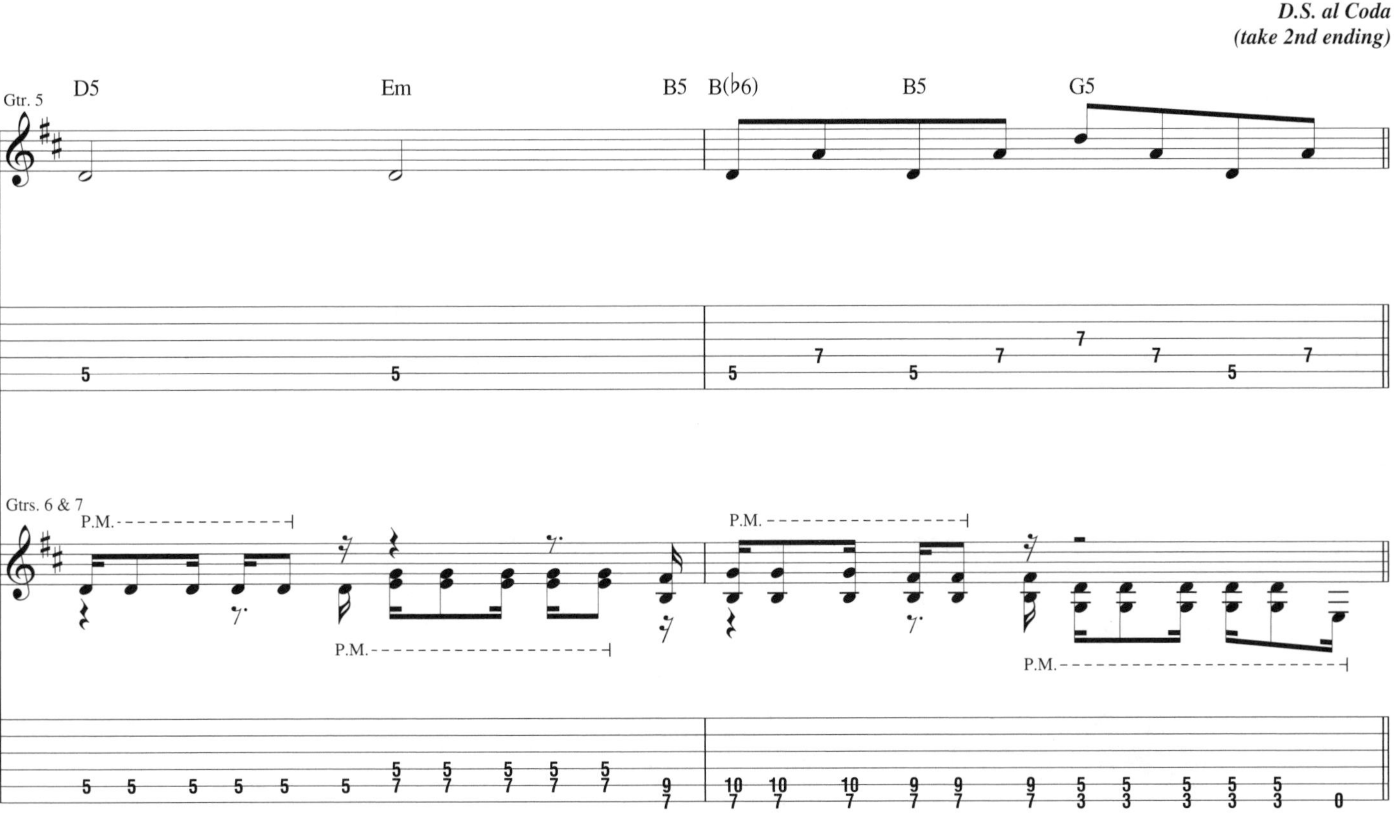
D.S. al Coda
(take 2nd ending)
Gtr. 5
D5
Em
B5 B(♭6)
B5
G5
Gtrs. 6 & 7
P.M.
P.M.
P.M.
P.M.

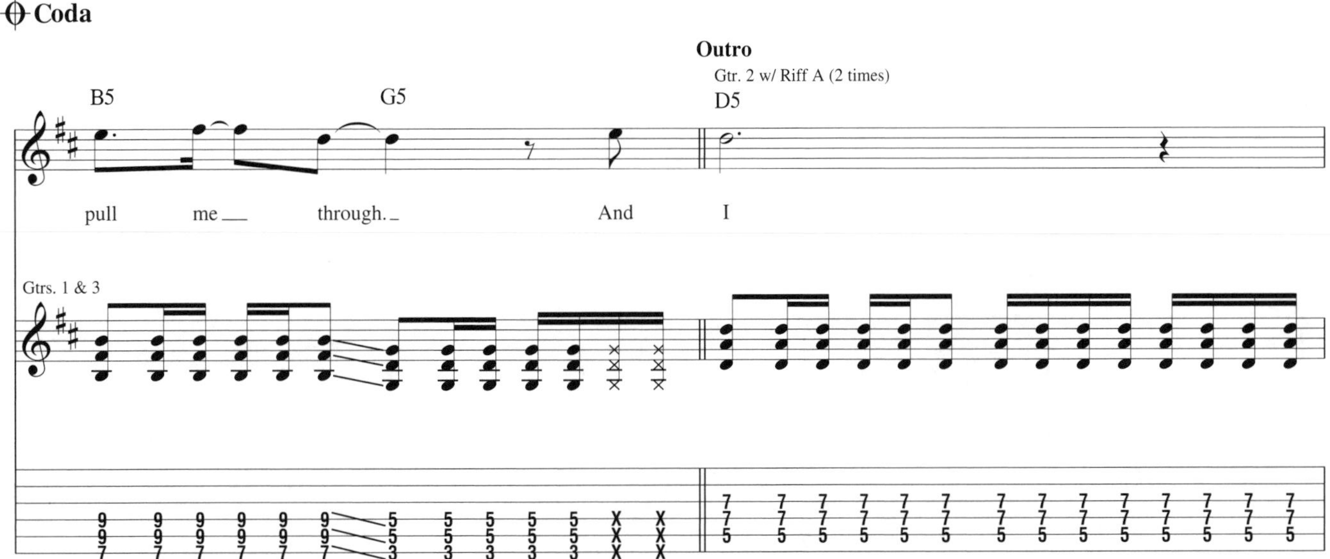
Coda
Outro
Gtr. 2 w/ Riff A (2 times)
B5
G5
D5
pull me through. And I
Gtrs. 1 & 3

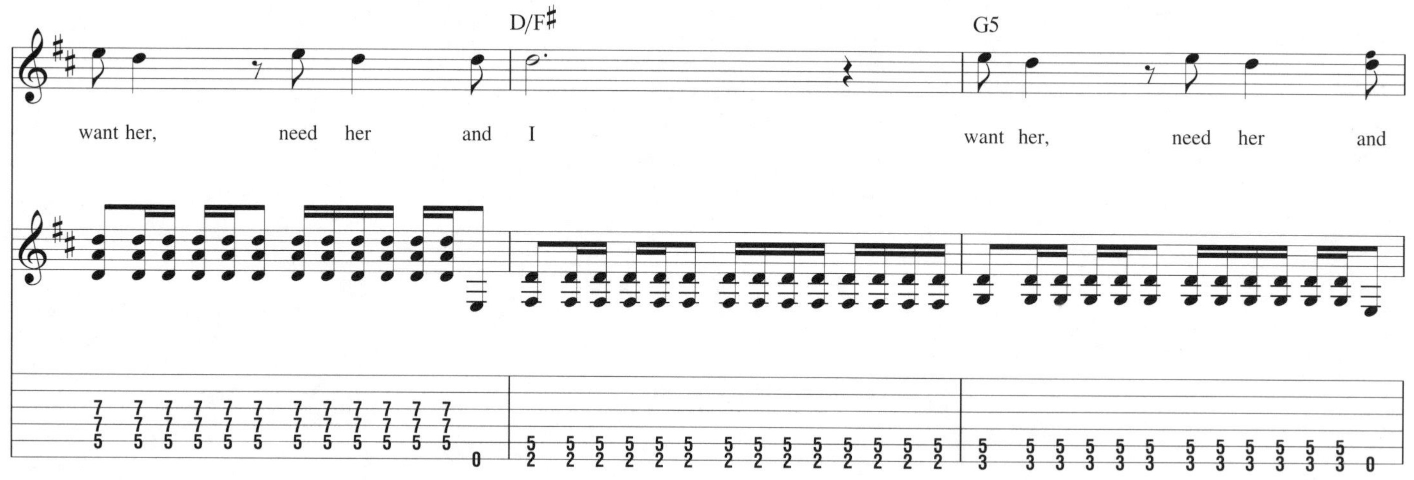
D/F♯
G5
want her, need her and I want her, need her and
7 7 7 7 7 7 7 7 7 7 7 7
7 7 7 7 7 7 7 7 7 7 7 7
5 5 5 5 5 5 5 5 5 5 5 5 0
5 5 5 5 5 5 5 5 5 5 5 5 5 5
2 2 2 2 2 2 2 2 2 2 2 2 2 2
5 5 5 5 5 5 5 5 5 5 5 5
3 3 3 3 3 3 3 3 3 3 3 3 0

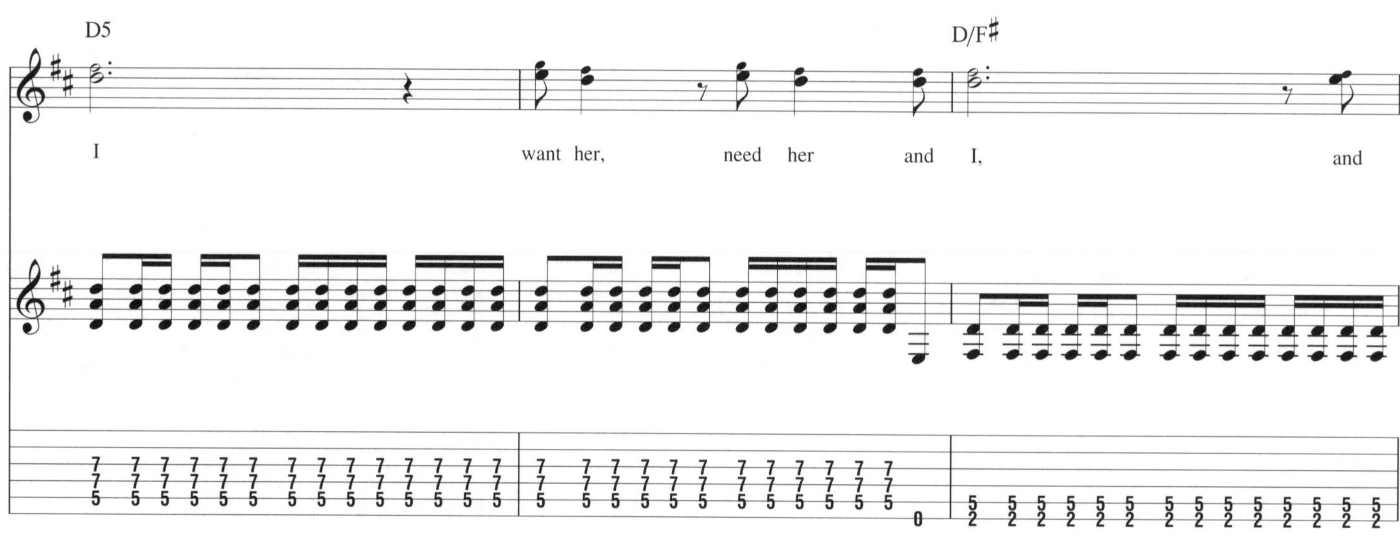
D5
D/F♯
I want her, need her and I, and
7 7 7 7 7 7 7 7 7 7 7 7 7 7
7 7 7 7 7 7 7 7 7 7 7 7 7 7
5 5 5 5 5 5 5 5 5 5 5 5 5 5
7 7 7 7 7 7 7 7 7 7 7 7
7 7 7 7 7 7 7 7 7 7 7 7
5 5 5 5 5 5 5 5 5 5 5 5 0
5 5 5 5 5 5 5 5 5 5 5 5 5 5
2 2 2 2 2 2 2 2 2 2 2 2 2 2

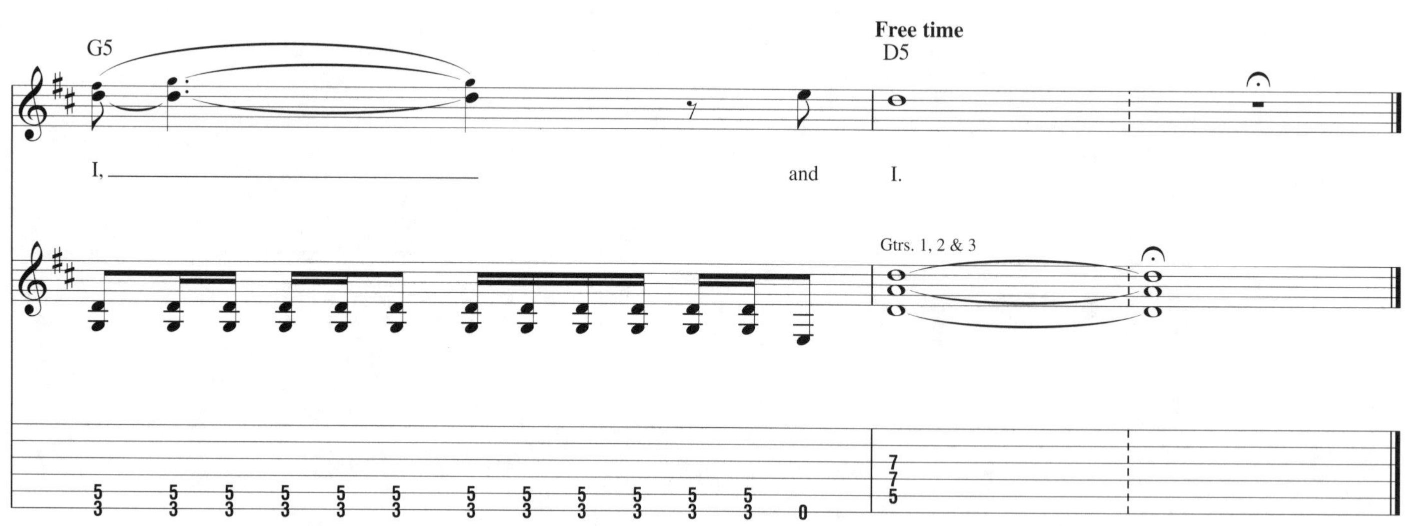
G5
Free time
D5
I, and I.
Gtrs. 1, 2 & 3
5 5 5 5 5 5 5 5 5 5 5 5
3 3 3 3 3 3 3 3 3 3 3 3 0
7
7
5

Letters to God

Words and Music by Tom De Longe and Travis Barker

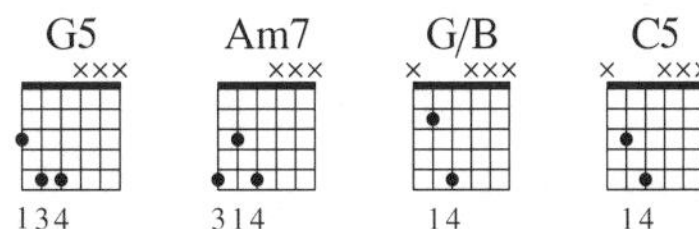

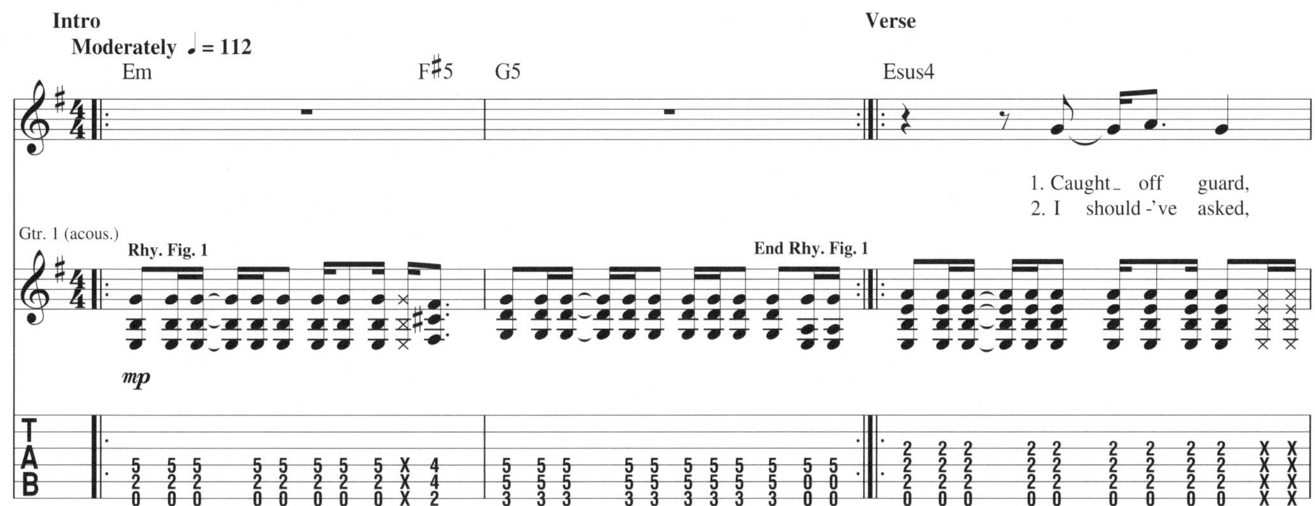

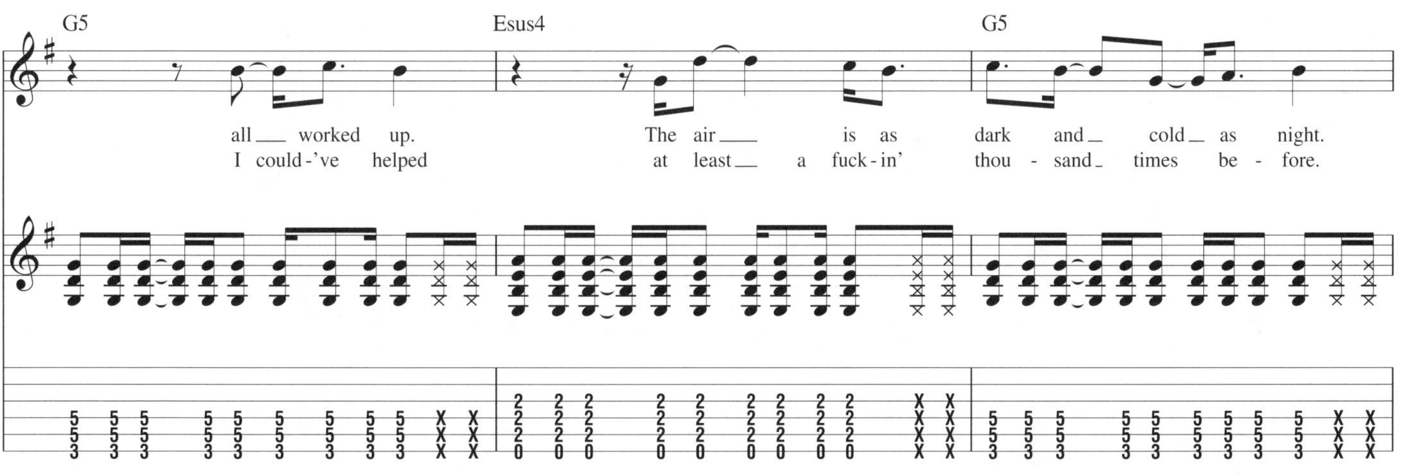

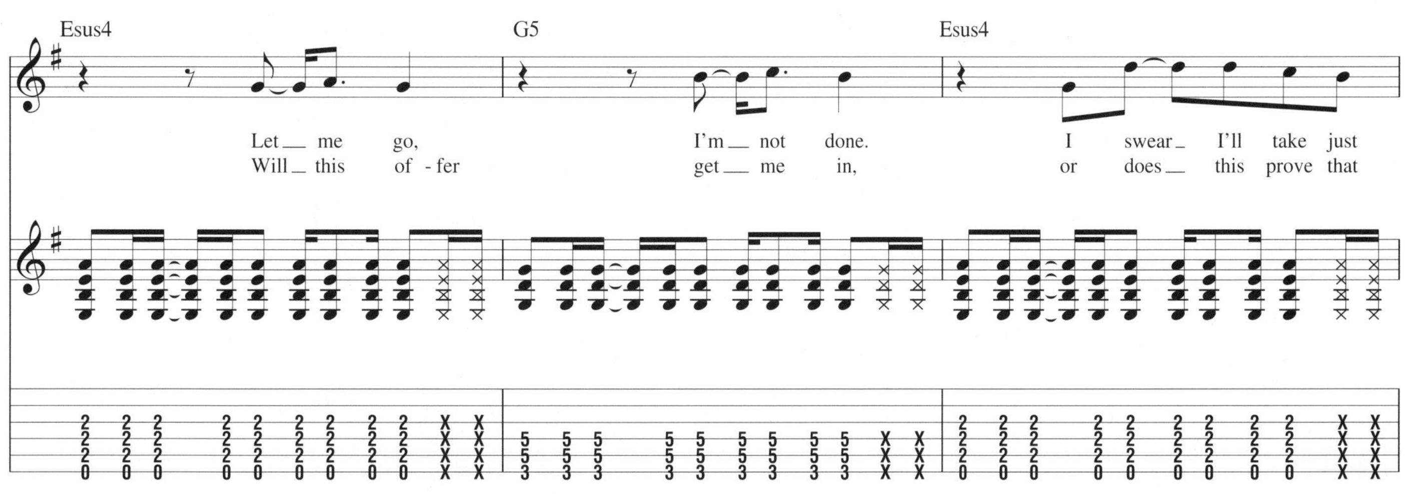

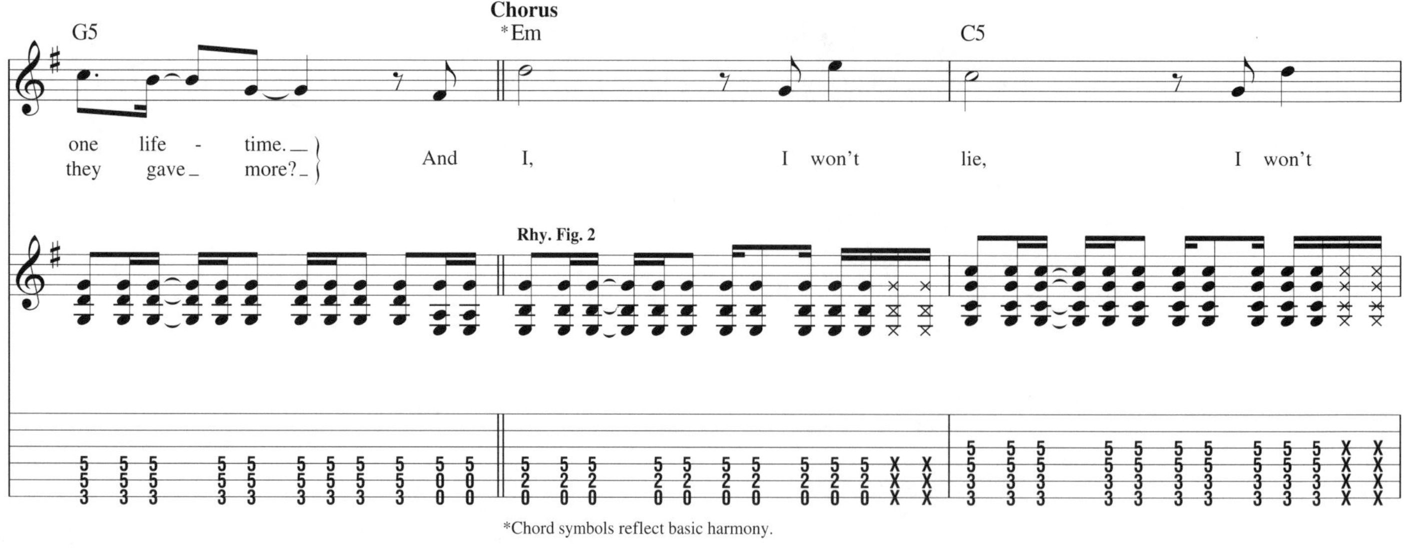

*Chord symbols reflect basic harmony.

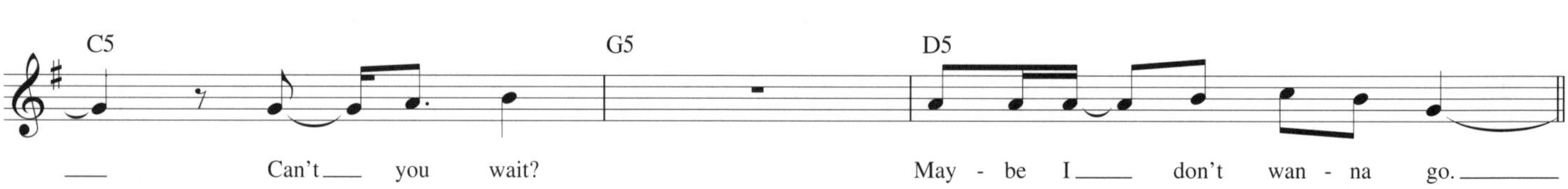

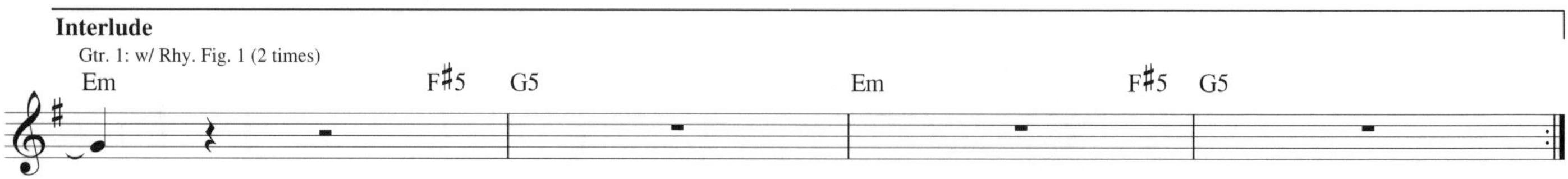

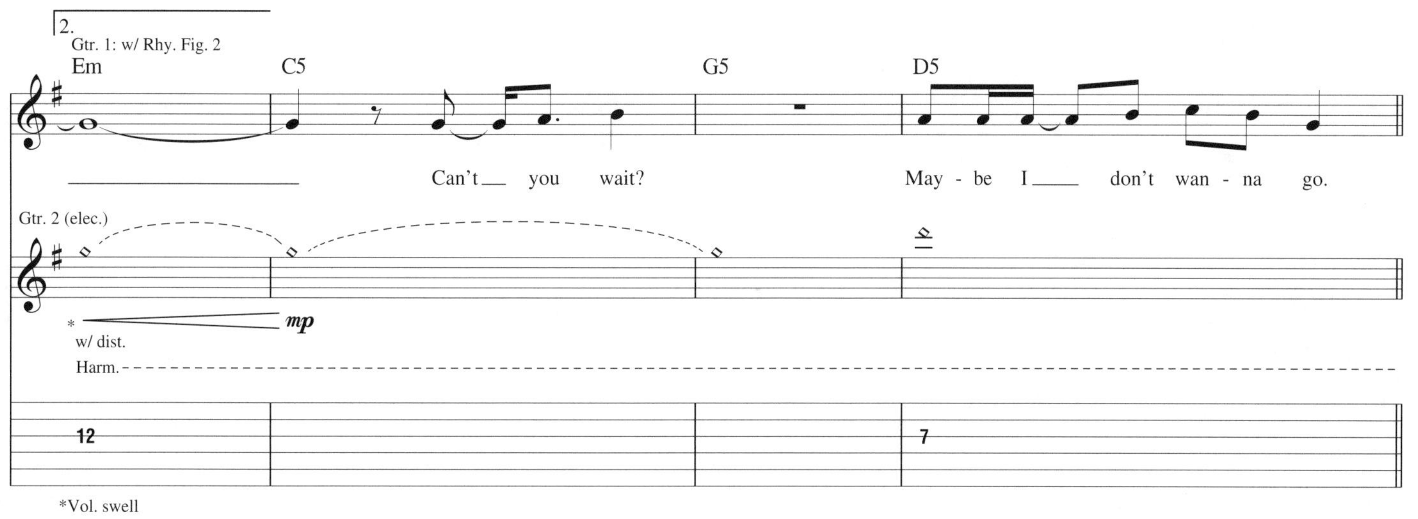
2.
Gtr. 1: w/ Rhy. Fig. 2
Em
C5
G5
D5
Can't you wait?
May - be I don't wan - na go.
Gtr. 2 (elec.)
mp
w/ dist.
Harm.
*Vol. swell

Interlude

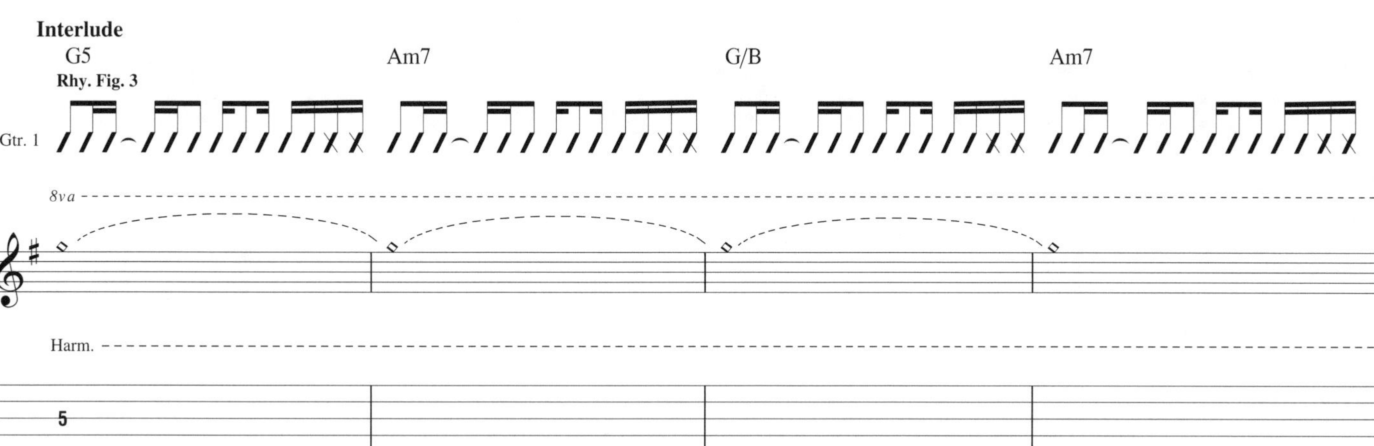
G5
Am7
G/B
Am7
Rhy. Fig. 3
Gtr. 1
8va
Harm.
Pitch: G

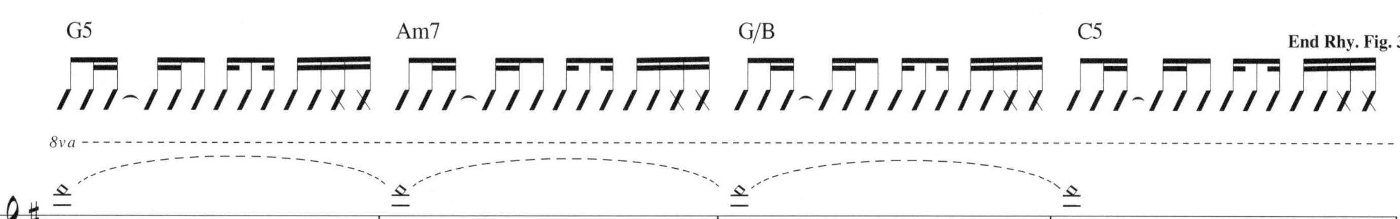
G5
Am7
G/B
C5
End Rhy. Fig. 3

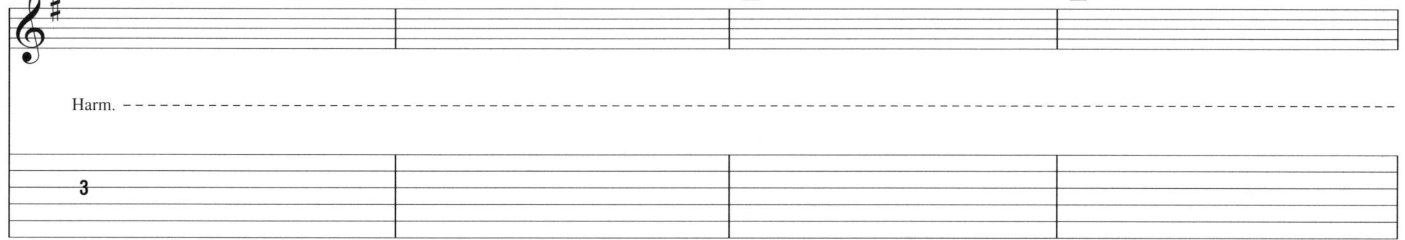
8va
Harm.
Pitch: D

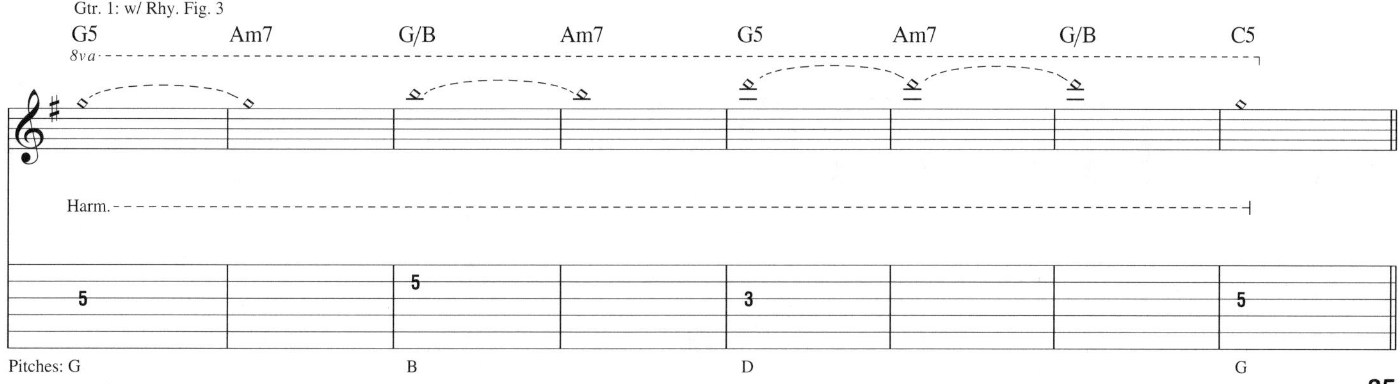
Gtr. 1: w/ Rhy. Fig. 3
G5
Am7
G/B
Am7
G5
Am7
G/B
C5
8va
Harm.
Pitches: G
B
D
G

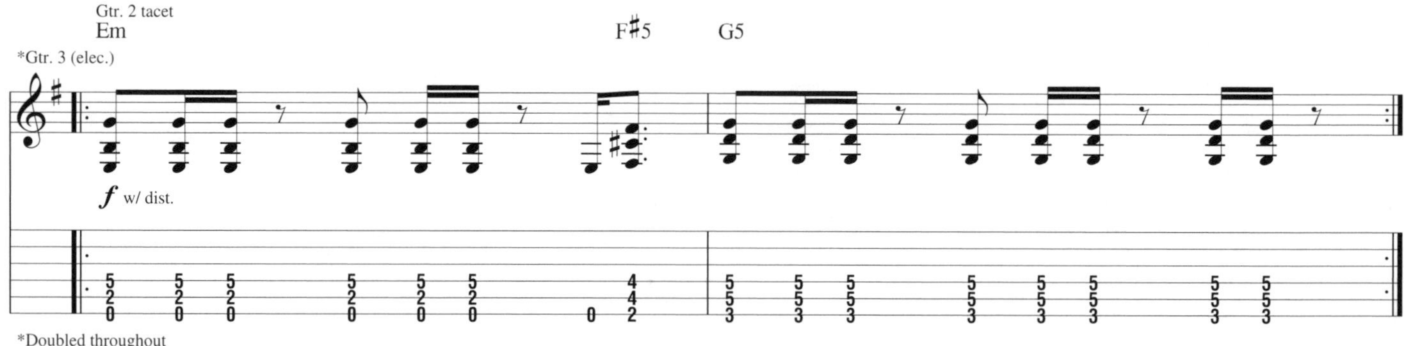

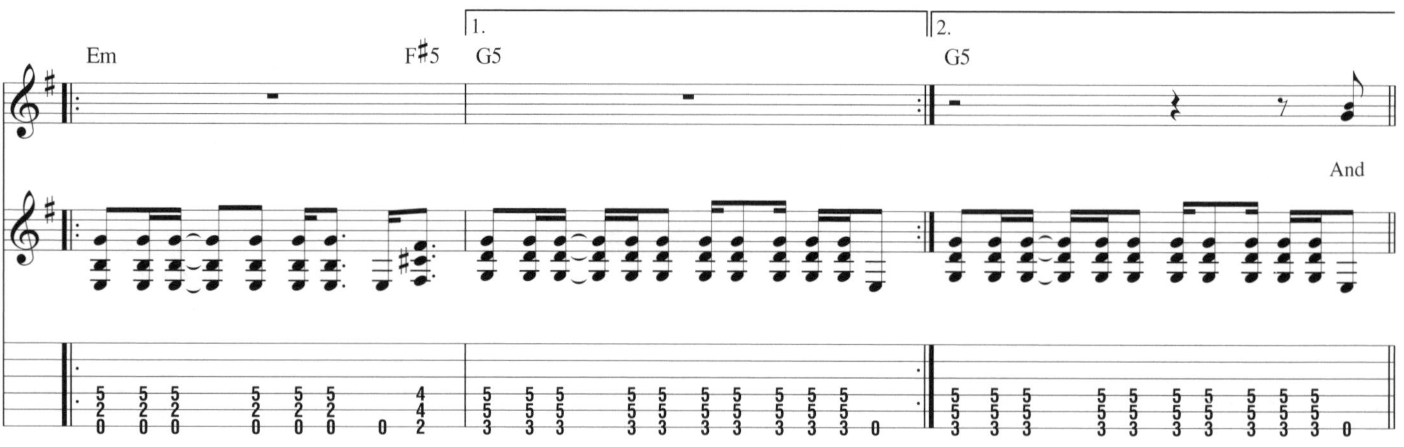

Outro-Chorus

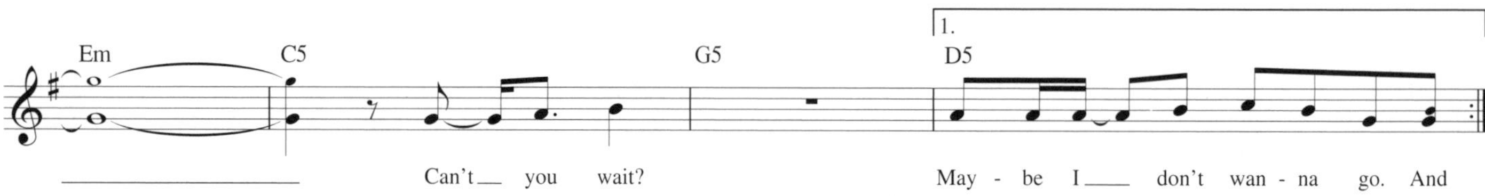

My First Punk Song

Words and Music by Tom De Longe and Travis Barker

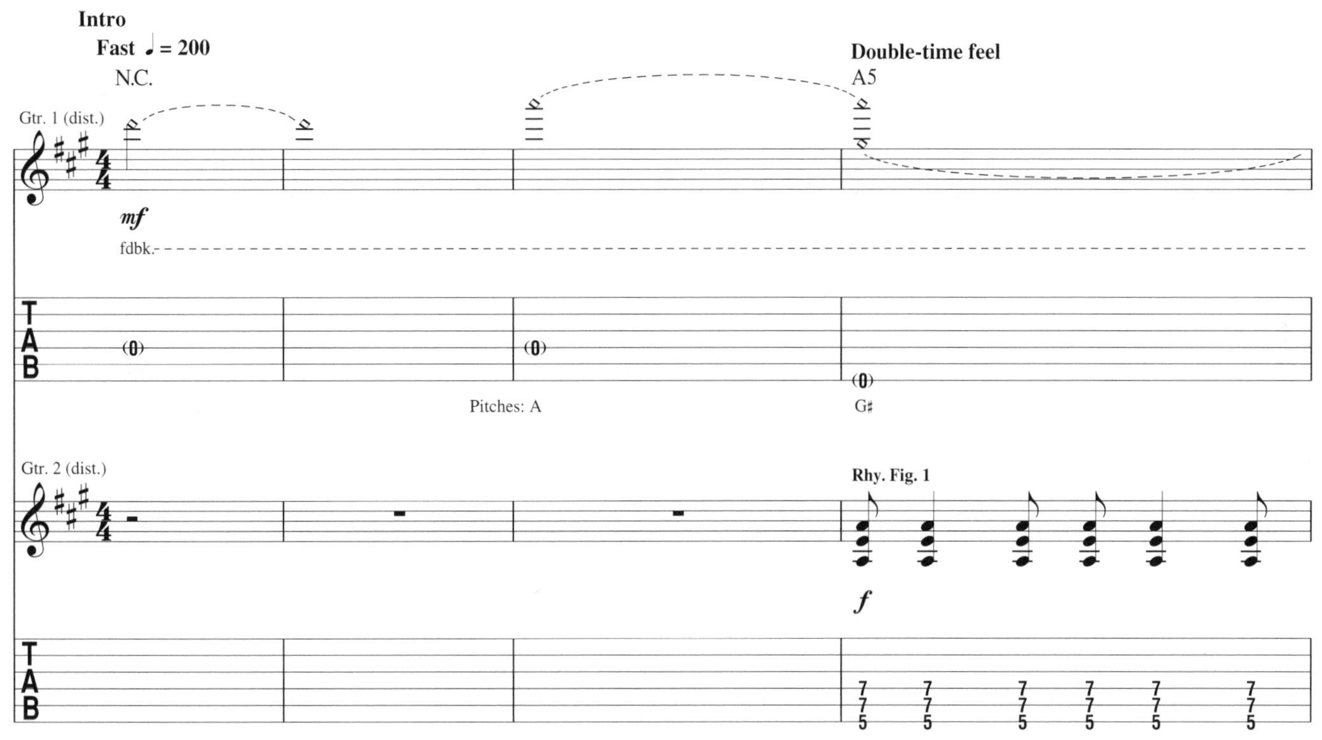

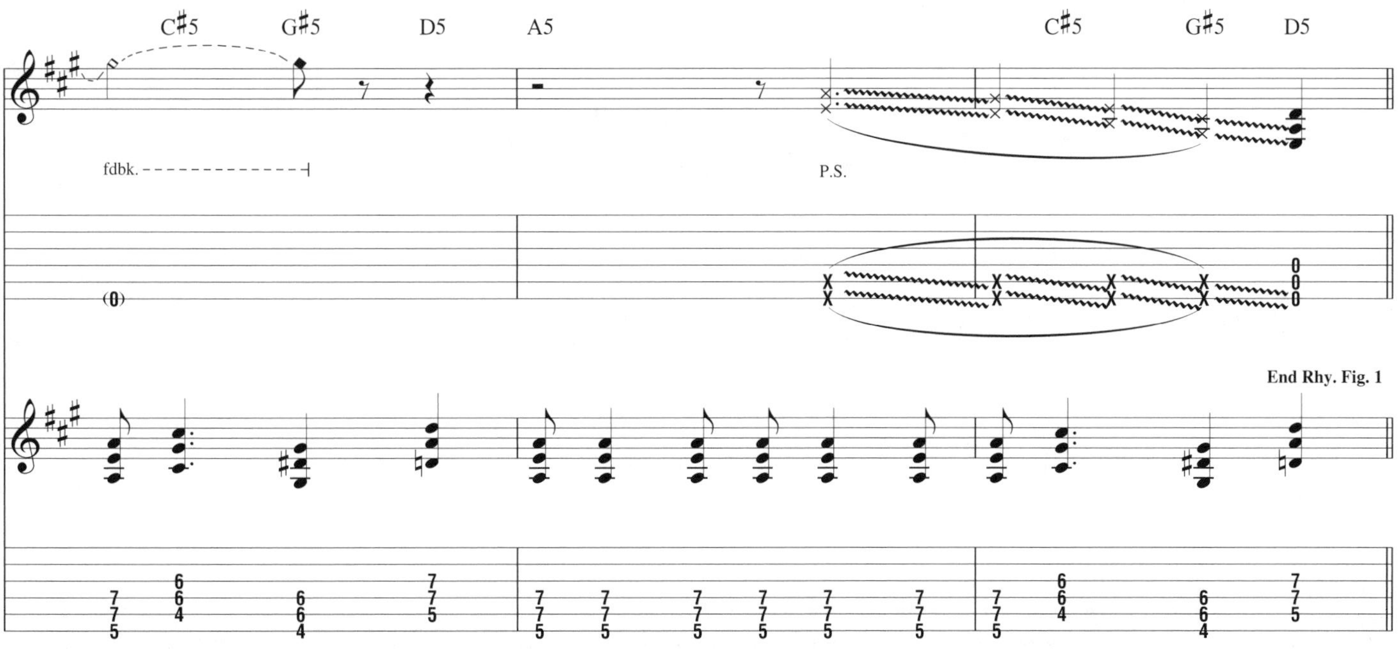

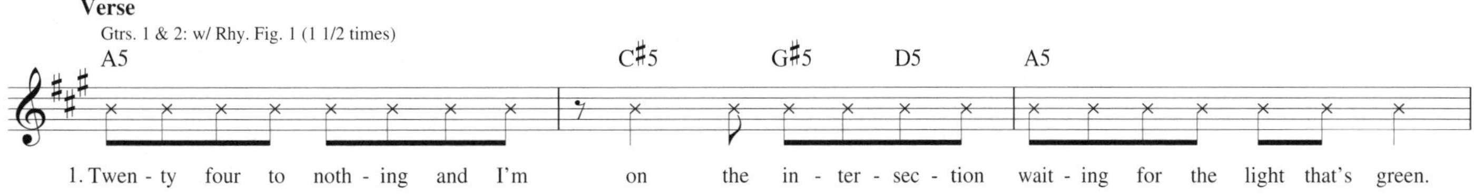

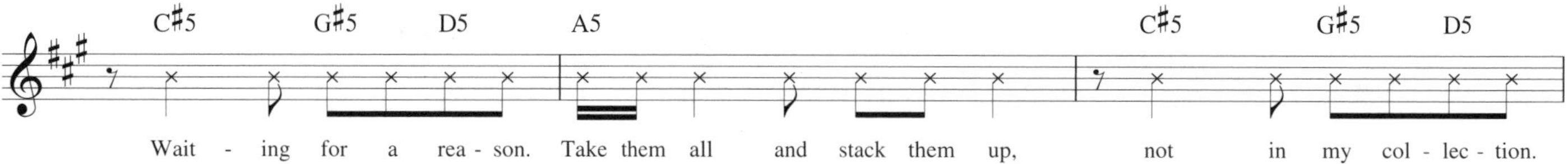
C♯5 G♯5 D5 A5 C♯5 G♯5 D5
Wait - ing for a rea - son. Take them all and stack them up, not in my col - lec - tion.

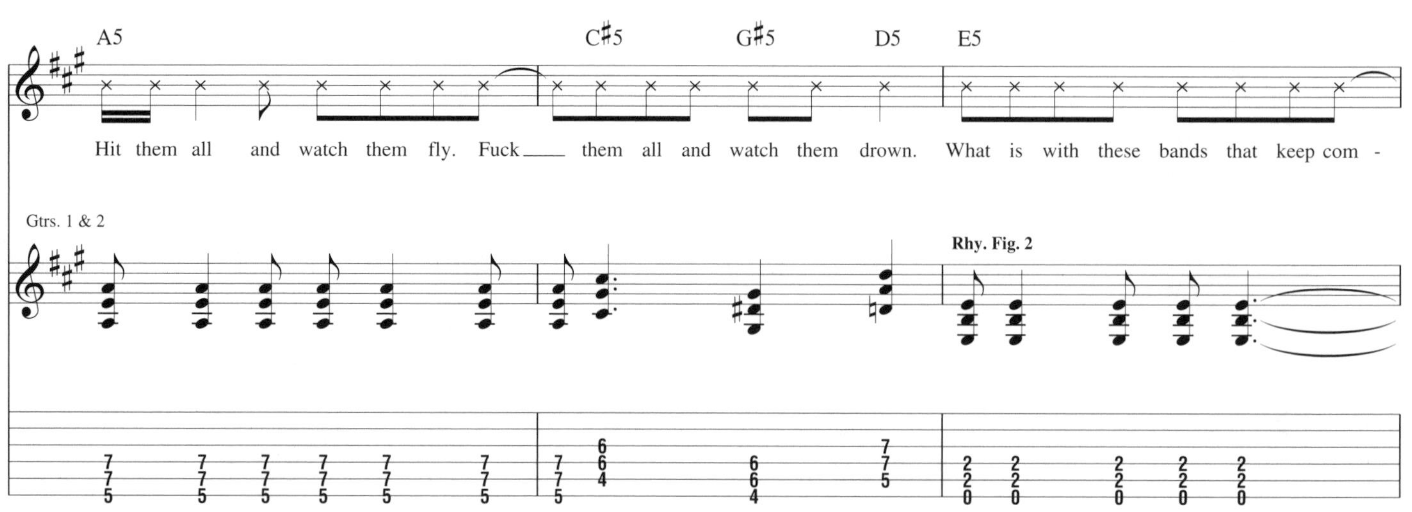
A5 C♯5 G♯5 D5 E5
Hit them all and watch them fly. Fuck them all and watch them drown. What is with these bands that keep com -
Gtrs. 1 & 2
Rhy. Fig. 2

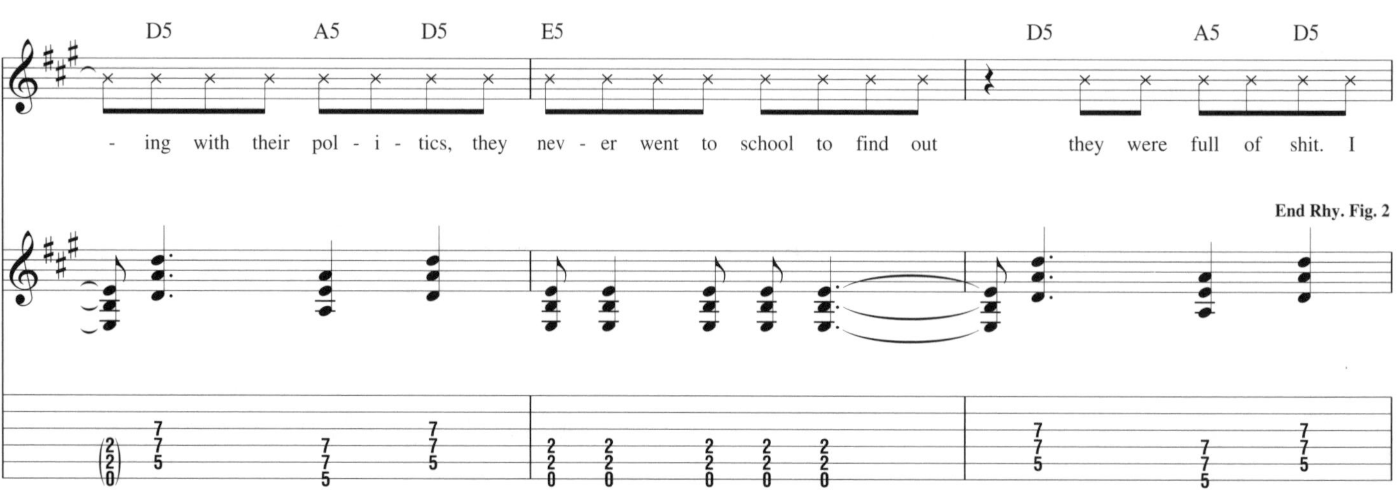
D5 A5 D5 E5 D5 A5 D5
- ing with their pol - i - tics, they nev - er went to school to find out they were full of shit. I
End Rhy. Fig. 2

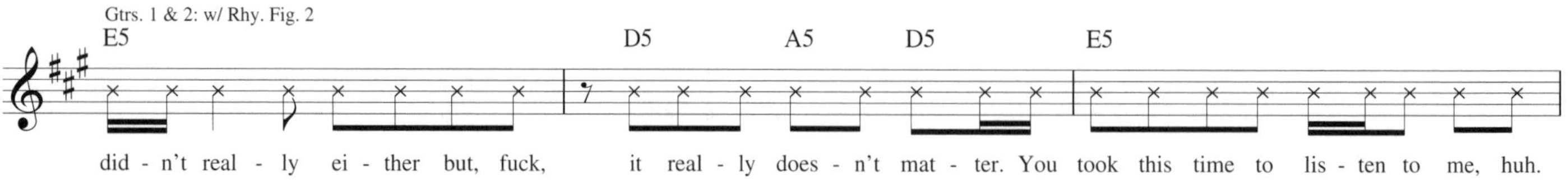
Gtrs. 1 & 2: w/ Rhy. Fig. 2
E5 D5 A5 D5 E5
did - n't real - ly ei - ther but, fuck, it real - ly does - n't mat - ter. You took this time to lis - ten to me, huh.

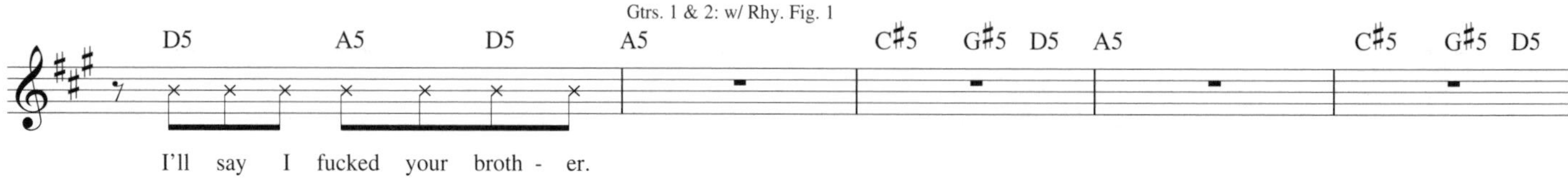
Gtrs. 1 & 2: w/ Rhy. Fig. 1
D5 A5 D5 A5 C♯5 G♯5 D5 A5 C♯5 G♯5 D5
I'll say I fucked your broth - er.

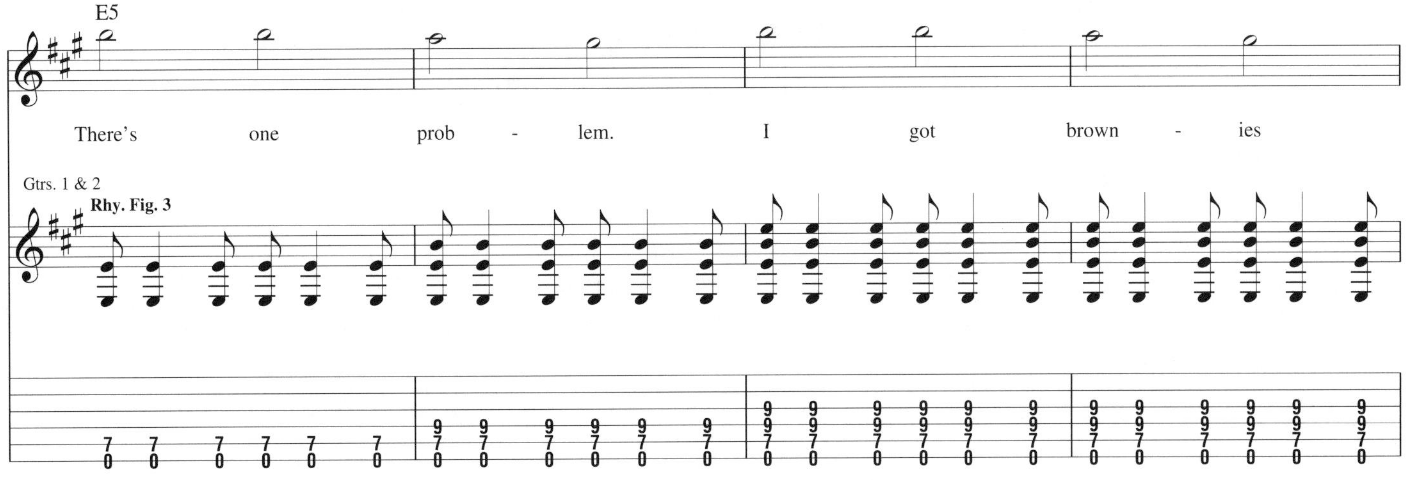
E5
There's one prob - lem. I got brown - ies
Gtrs. 1 & 2
Rhy. Fig. 3

G♯5
from your moth - er. It gave me syph - i - lis. Spoken: I
End Rhy. Fig. 3

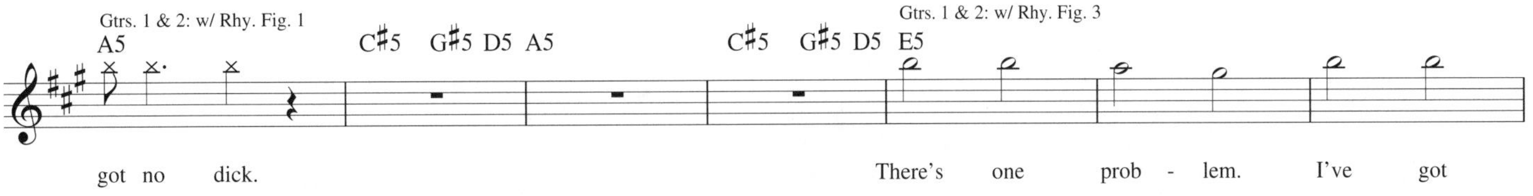
Gtrs. 1 & 2: w/ Rhy. Fig. 1
A5
C♯5 G♯5 D5 A5
C♯5 G♯5 D5
Gtrs. 1 & 2: w/ Rhy. Fig. 3
E5
got no dick.
There's one prob - lem. I've got

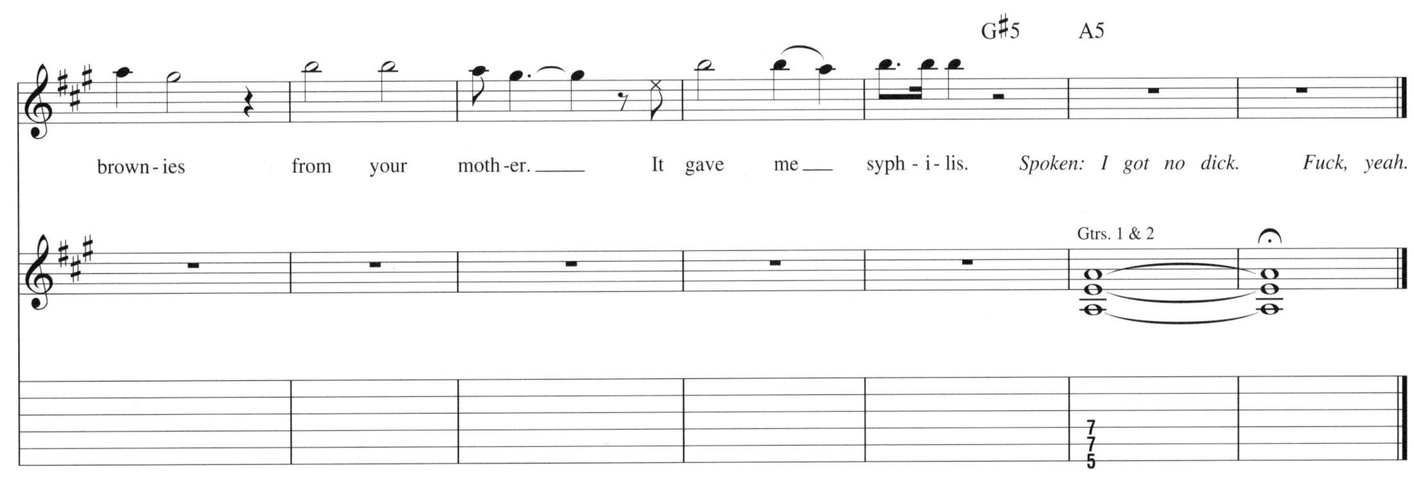
G♯5 A5
brown - ies from your moth - er. It gave me syph - i - lis. Spoken: I got no dick. Fuck, yeah.
Gtrs. 1 & 2

Sorrow

Words and Music by Tom De Longe and Travis Barker

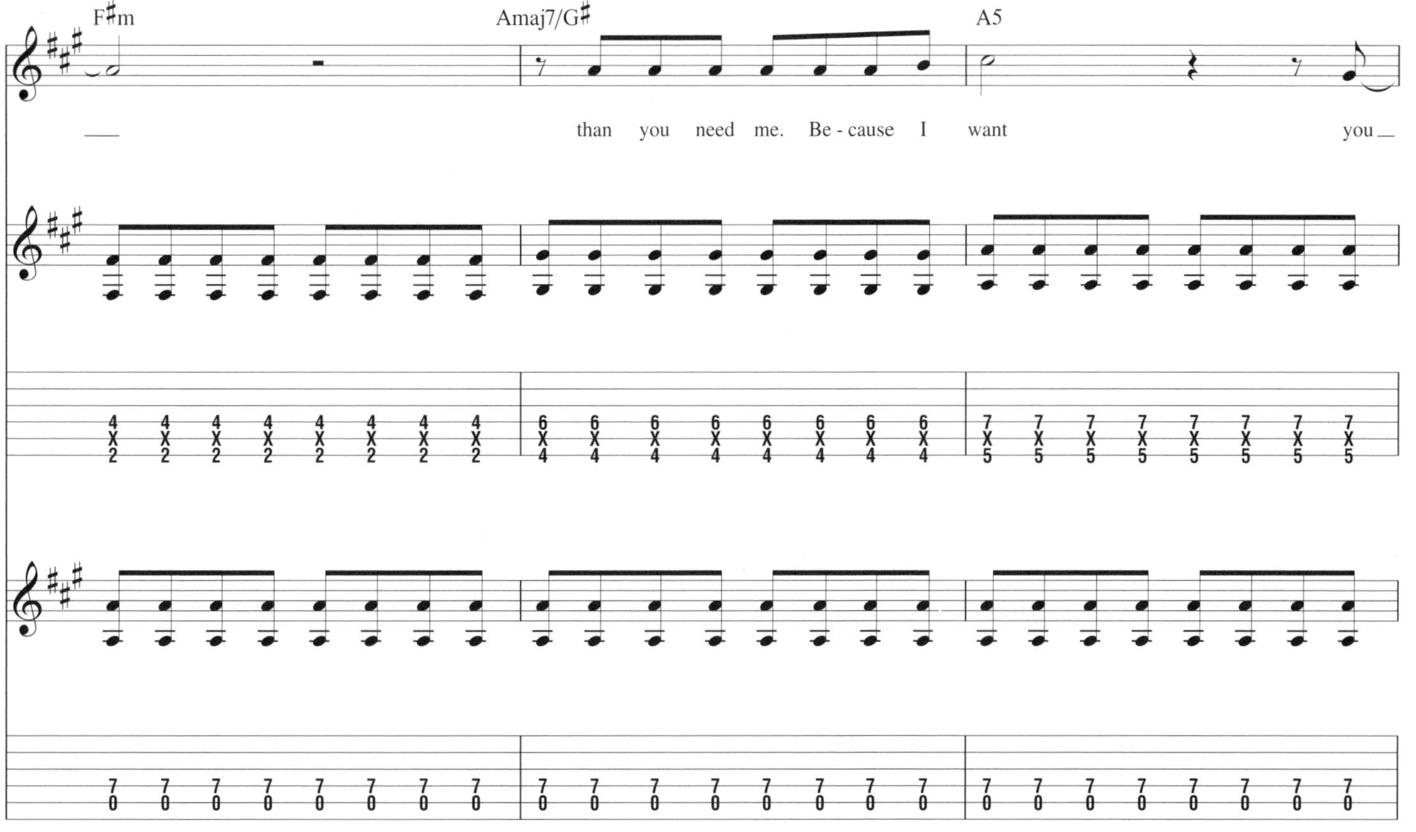
F♯m
Amaj7/G♯
A5
than you need me. Be - cause I want you

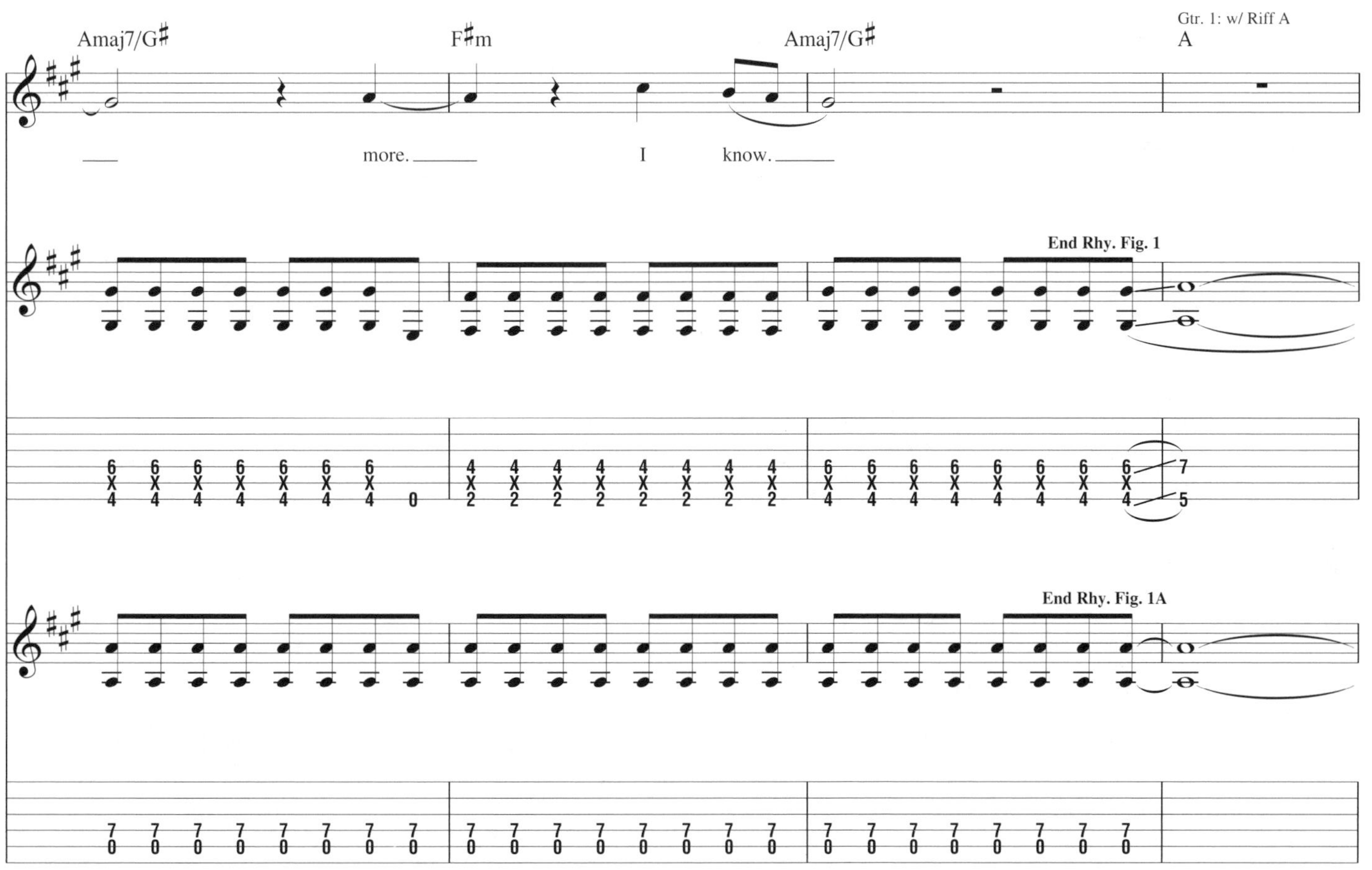
Amaj7/G♯
F♯m
Amaj7/G♯
Gtr. 1: w/ Riff A
A
more. I know.
End Rhy. Fig. 1
End Rhy. Fig. 1A

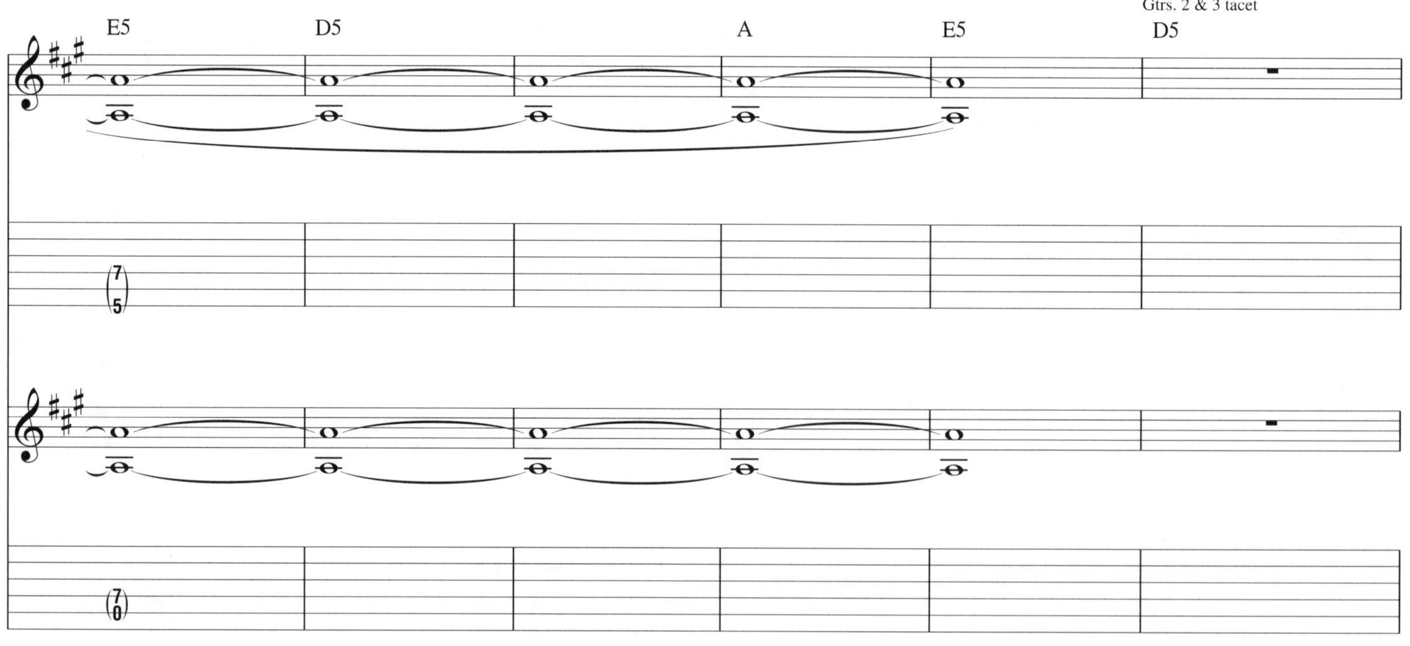
Gtrs. 2 & 3 tacet
E5
D5
A
E5
D5
7
5
7
0

Verse
Gtrs. 2 & 3: w/ Rhy. Figs. 1 & 1A
A5
Amaj7/G♯
F♯m
2. Be - cause we move too fuck - ing fast.

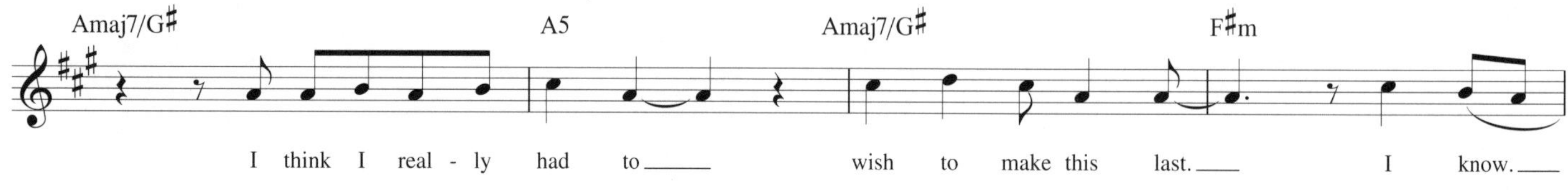
Amaj7/G♯
A5
Amaj7/G♯
F♯m
I think I real - ly had to wish to make this last. I know.

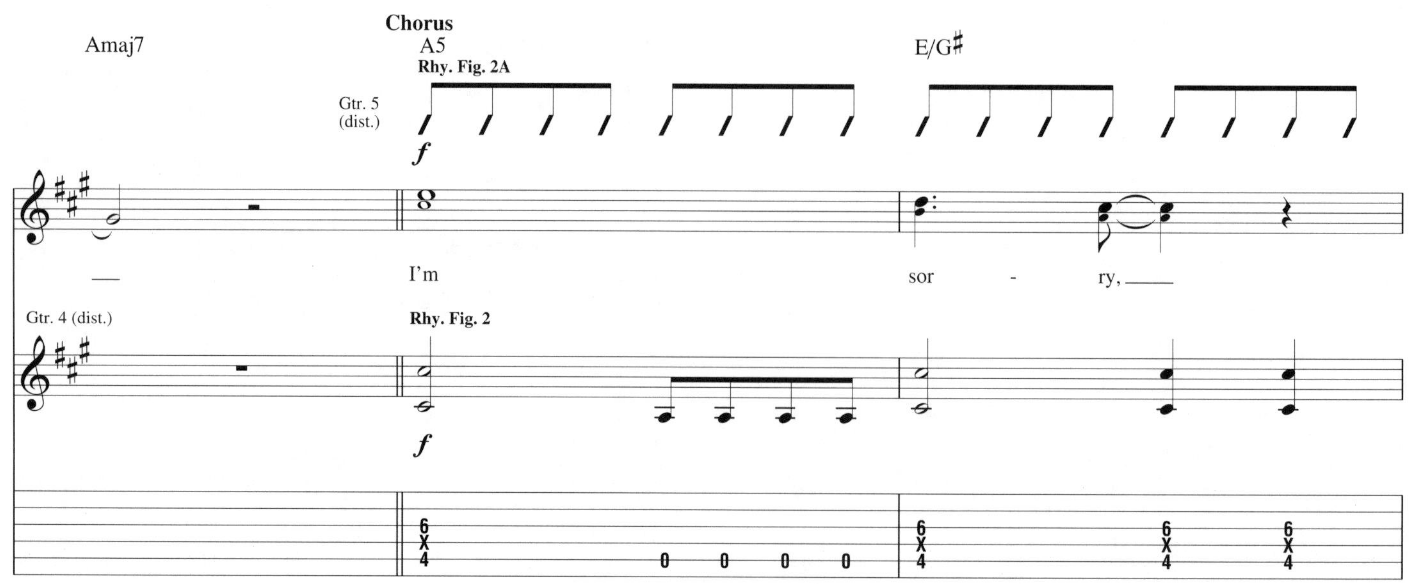
Chorus
Amaj7
A5
E/G♯
Rhy. Fig. 2A
Gtr. 5 (dist.)
f
I'm sor - ry,
Gtr. 4 (dist.)
Rhy. Fig. 2
f

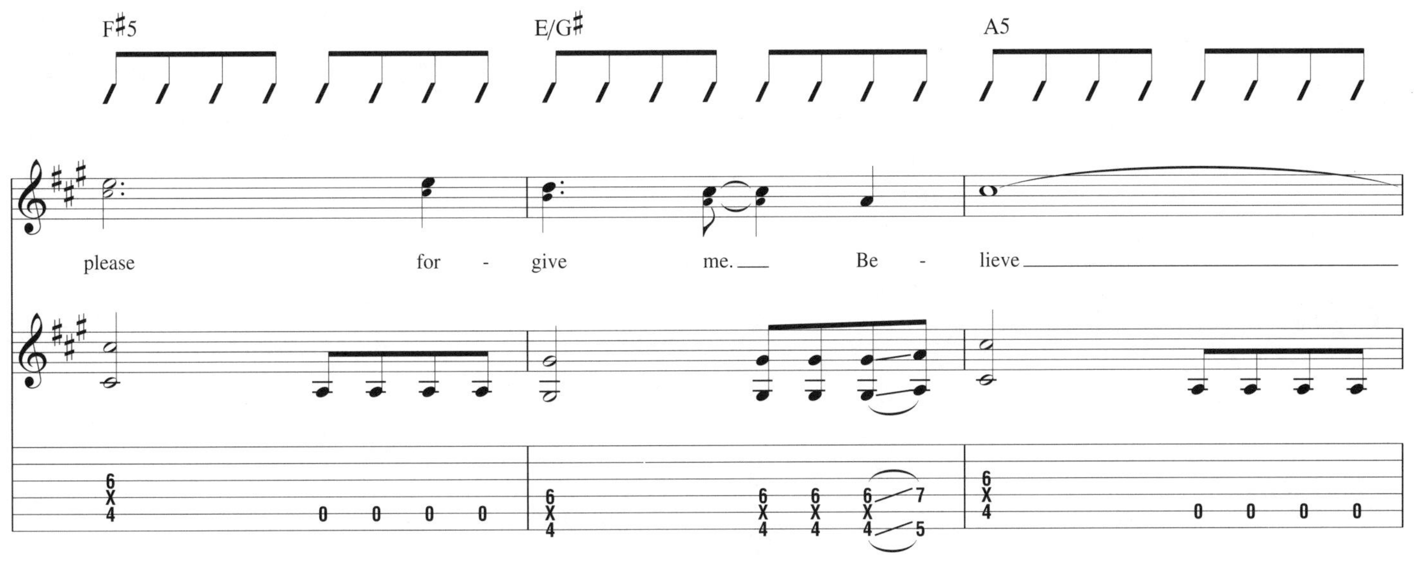
F♯5
E/G♯
A5
please for - give me. Be - lieve

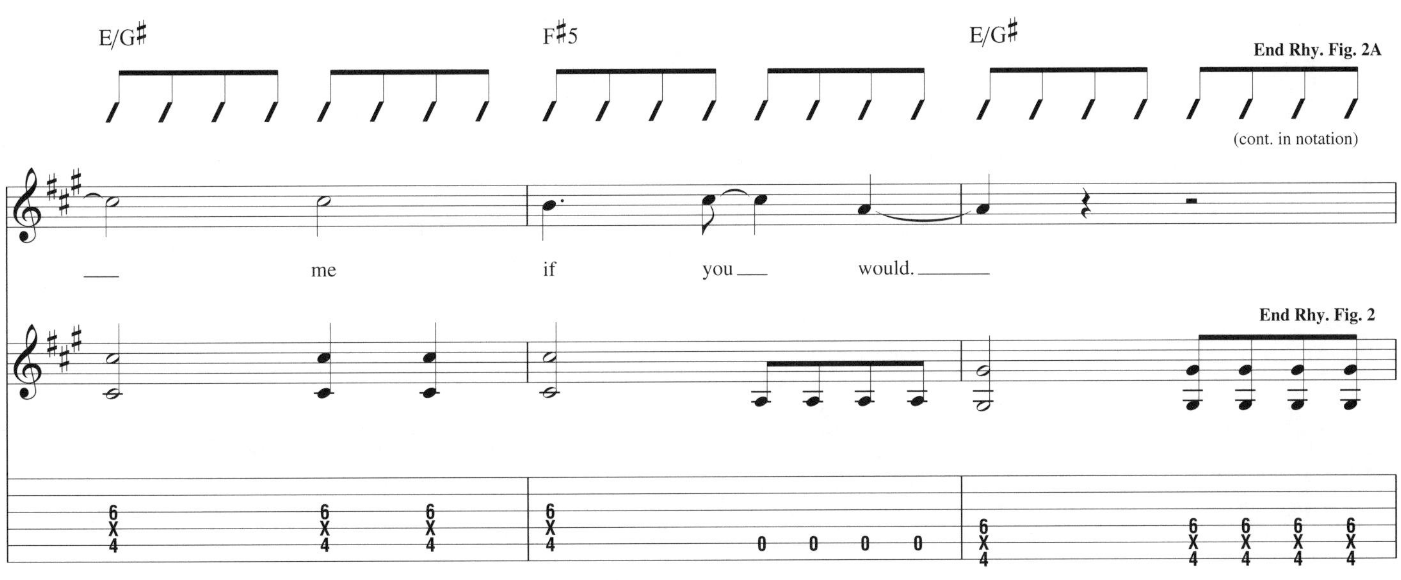
E/G♯
F♯5
E/G♯
End Rhy. Fig. 2A
(cont. in notation)
me if you would.
End Rhy. Fig. 2

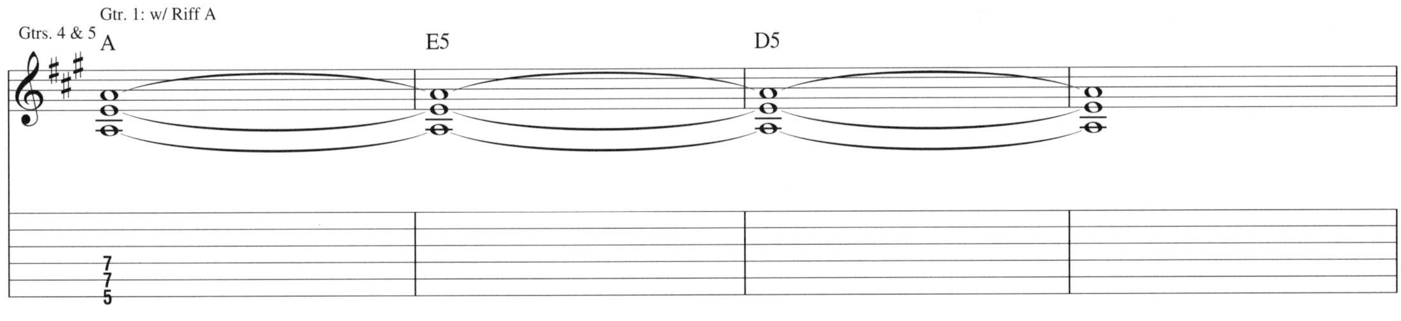
Gtr. 1: w/ Riff A
Gtrs. 4 & 5
A
E5
D5

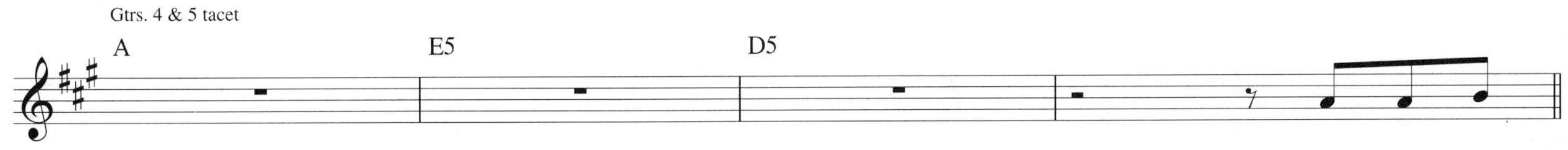
Gtrs. 4 & 5 tacet
A
E5
D5
3. Be - cause I

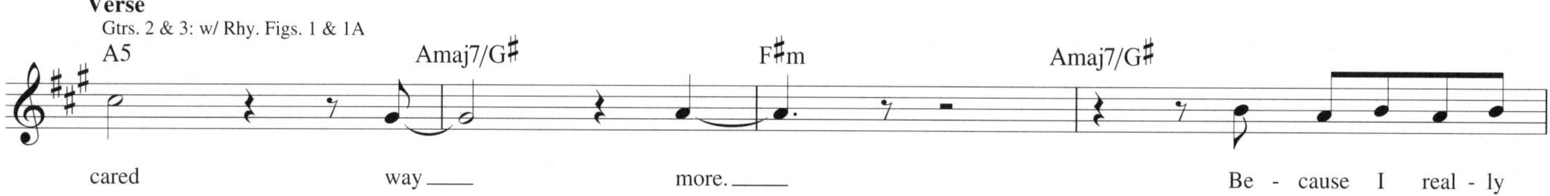
Verse
Gtrs. 2 & 3: w/ Rhy. Figs. 1 & 1A
A5
Amaj7/G♯
F♯m
Amaj7/G♯
cared way more. Be - cause I real - ly

A
Amaj7/G♯
F♯m
Amaj7/G♯
felt that you felt so much more. I know.

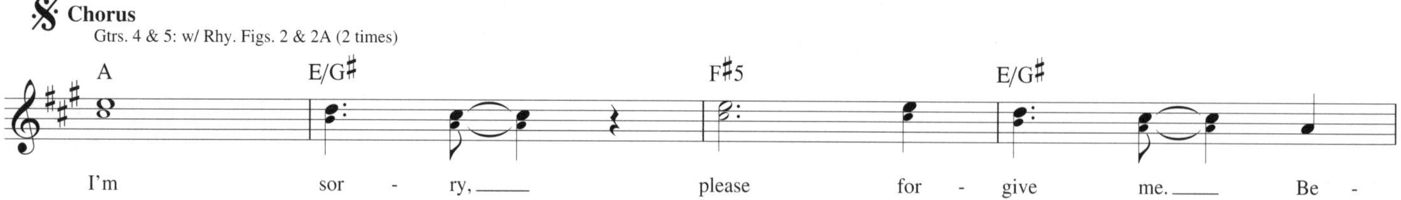
Chorus
Gtrs. 4 & 5: w/ Rhy. Figs. 2 & 2A (2 times)
A
E/G♯
F♯5
E/G♯
I'm sor - ry, please for - give me. Be -

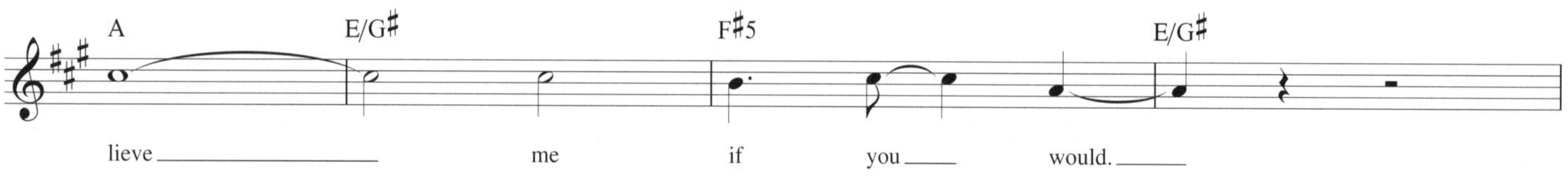
A
E/G♯
F♯5
E/G♯
lieve me if you would.

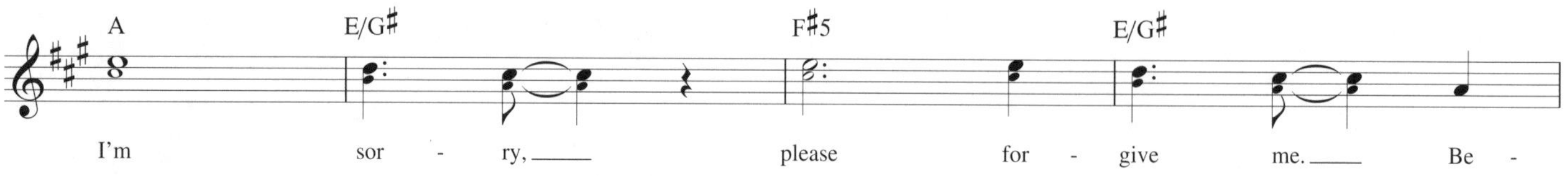
A
E/G♯
F♯5
E/G♯
I'm sor - ry, please for - give me. Be -

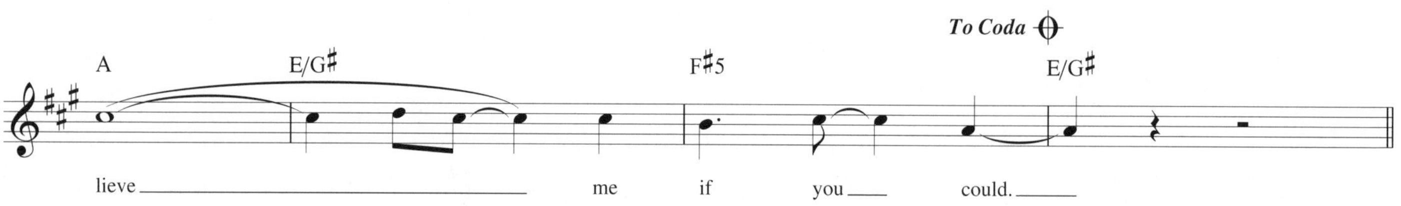
To Coda
A
E/G♯
F♯5
E/G♯
lieve me if you could.

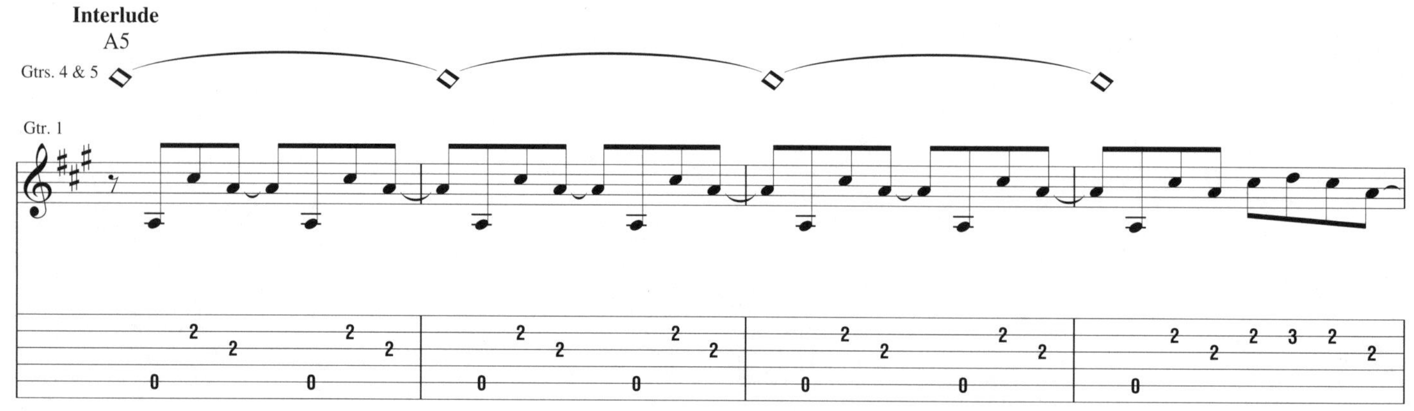
Interlude
A5
Gtrs. 4 & 5
Gtr. 1

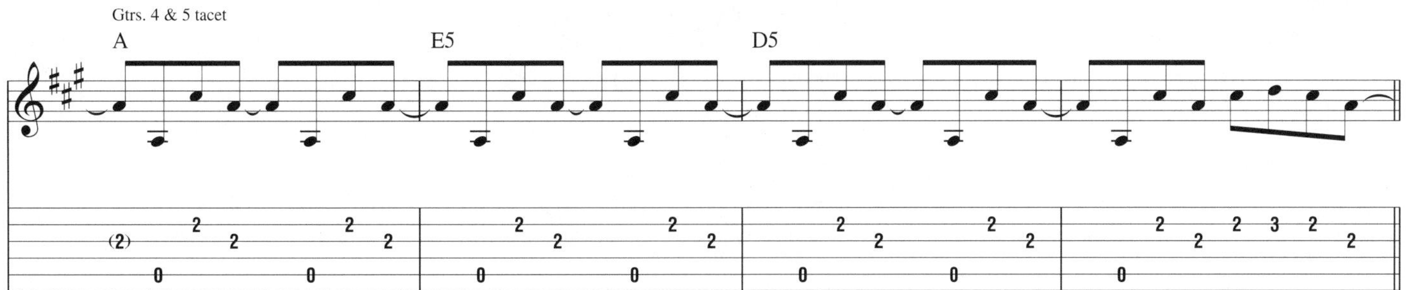

D.S. al Coda

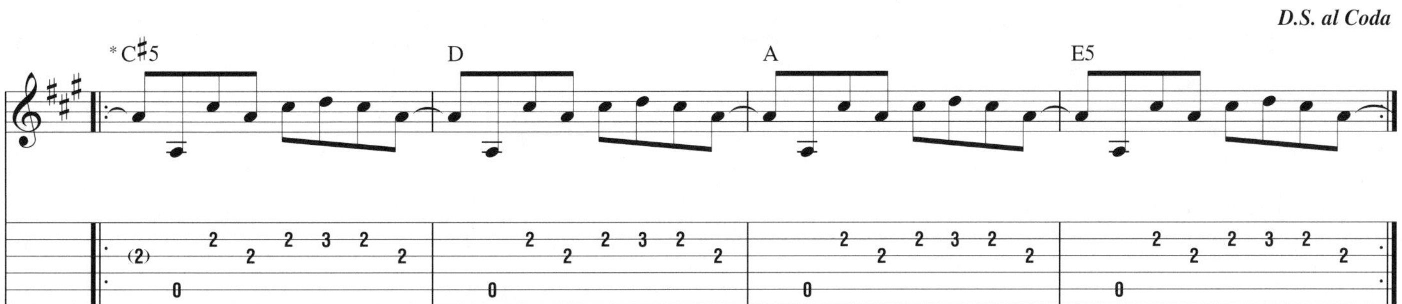

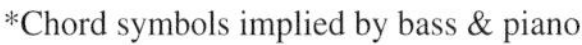
*Chord symbols implied by bass & piano.

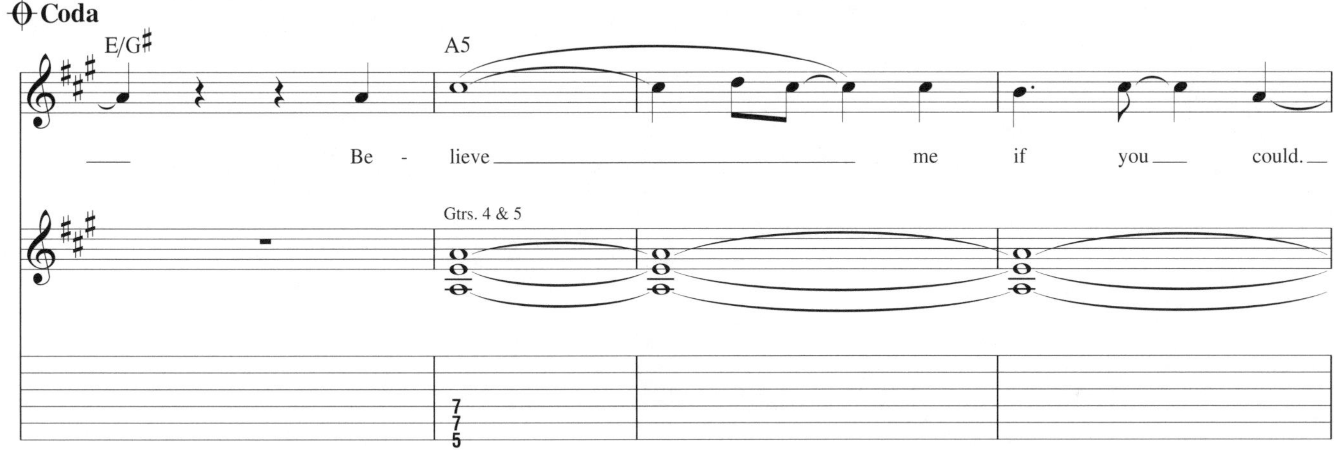

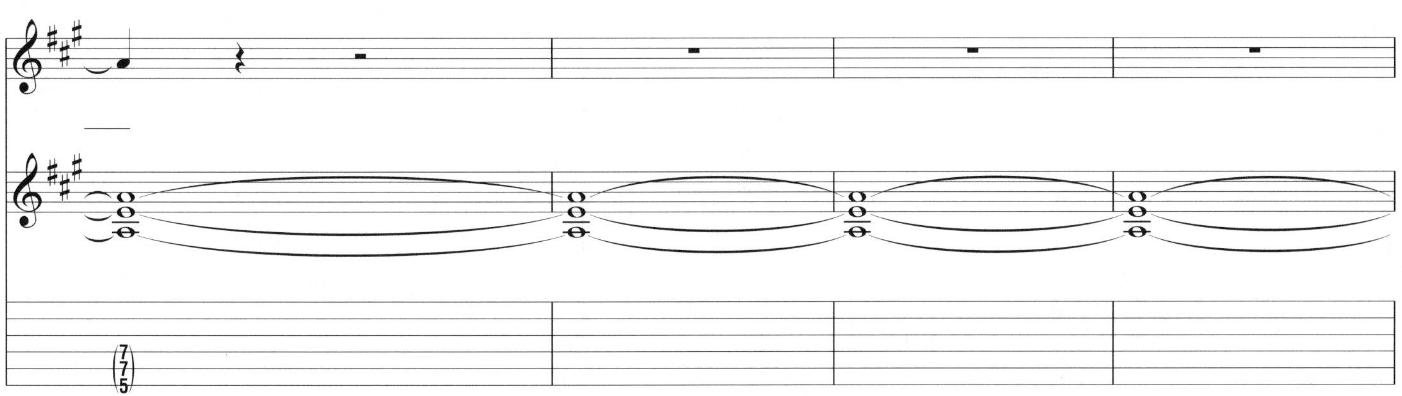

There Is

Words and Music by Tom De Longe and Travis Barker

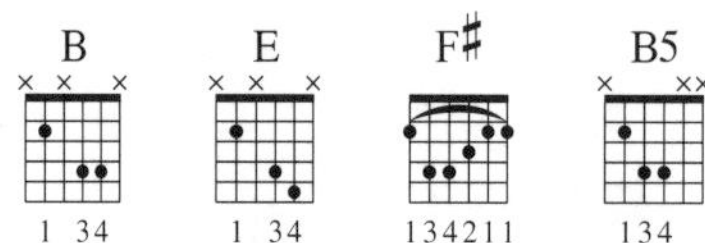

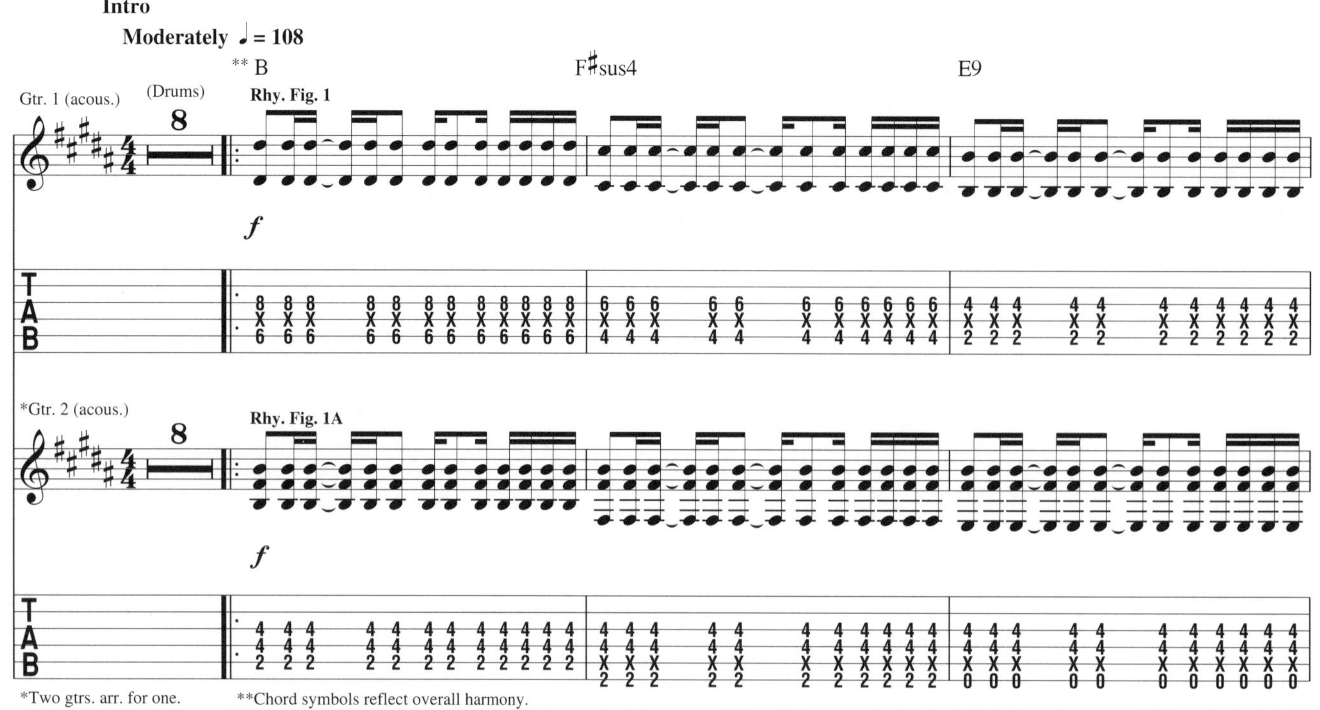

*Two gtrs. arr. for one. **Chord symbols reflect overall harmony.

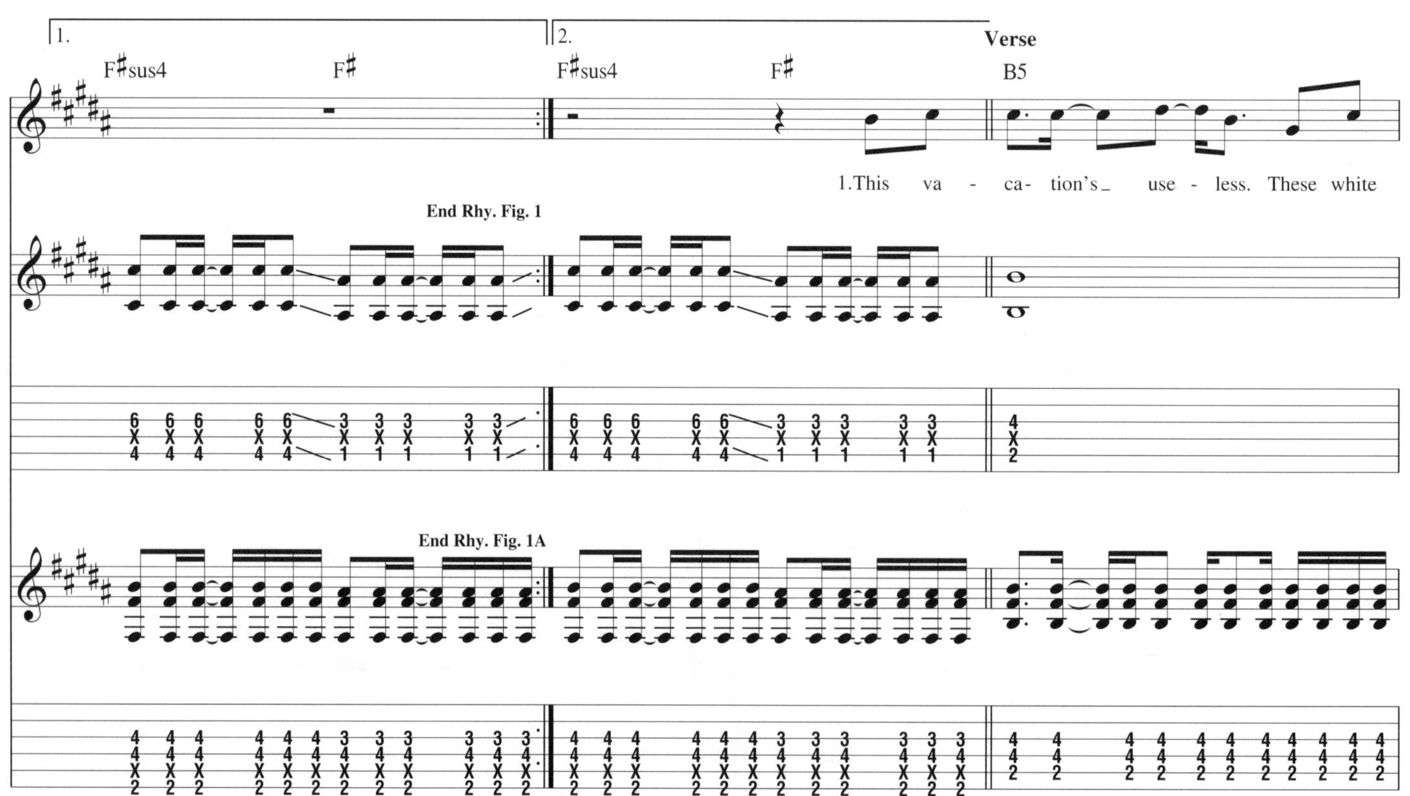

Gtr. 1 tacet
B7
G♯m7
E5
pills aren't kind. I've given a lot of thought on this thirteen hour drive. I've
Gtr. 2
B5
B7
G♯m7
missed the grinding concrete where we sat past eight or nine and slowly finished laughing in the
E5
B5
F♯sus4
glow of our headlights. I've given a lot of thought to the nights we used to have. The
Rhy. Fig. 2
G♯m7
E5
Gtr. 2: w/ Rhy. Fig. 2
B5
days have come and gone. Our lives went by so fast. I faintly remember breathing
End Rhy. Fig. 2

F#sus4 G#m7 E5

on your bed - room floor where I laid and told you but you sweared you loved me more. Do you

Chorus

Gtr. 2: w/ Rhy. Fig. 2

B5 F#sus4 G#m7 E5

care if I don't know what to say? Will you sleep to - night? Will you think of me? Will I

Gtr. 3 (elec.)

Riff A

mf

w/ clean tone

B5 F#sus4 G#m7

shake this off, pre - tend it's all O. - K. that there's some - one out there who feels

Gtr. 2

Rhy. Fig. 3

Gtr. 3

Gtr. 1: w/ Rhy. Fig. 1

Gtr. 2: w/ Rhy. Fig. 1A

F#sus4 B F#sus4

just like me? There is.

End Rhy. Fig. 3

End Riff A

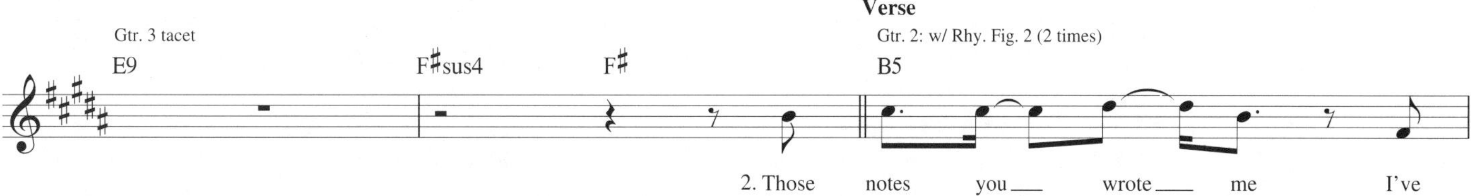
Gtr. 3 tacet
Verse
Gtr. 2: w/ Rhy. Fig. 2 (2 times)
E9
F♯sus4
F♯
B5
2. Those notes you wrote me I've

F♯sus4
G♯m7
E5
kept them all. I've giv - en a lot of thought of how to write you back this fall. With

B5
F♯sus4
G♯m7
ev - 'ry sin - gle let - ter in ev - 'ry sin - gle word there will be a hid - den mes - sage a - bout a

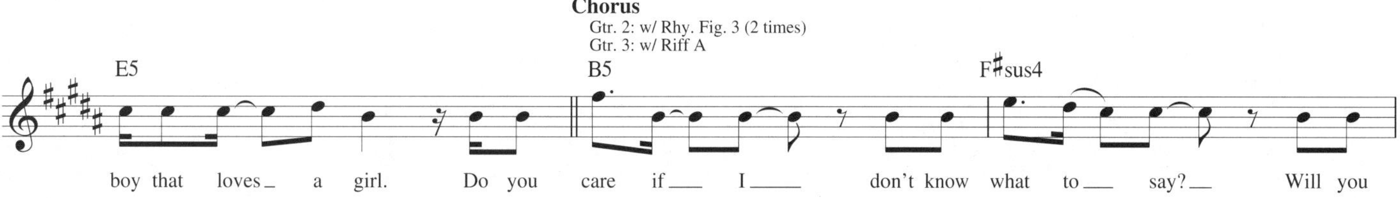
Chorus
Gtr. 2: w/ Rhy. Fig. 3 (2 times)
Gtr. 3: w/ Riff A
E5
B5
F♯sus4
boy that loves a girl. Do you care if I don't know what to say? Will you

G♯m7
F♯sus4
B5
sleep to - night or will you think of me? Will I shake this off, pre - tend it's

F♯sus4
G♯m7
F♯sus4
all O. - K. that there's some - one out there who feels just like me? There is.

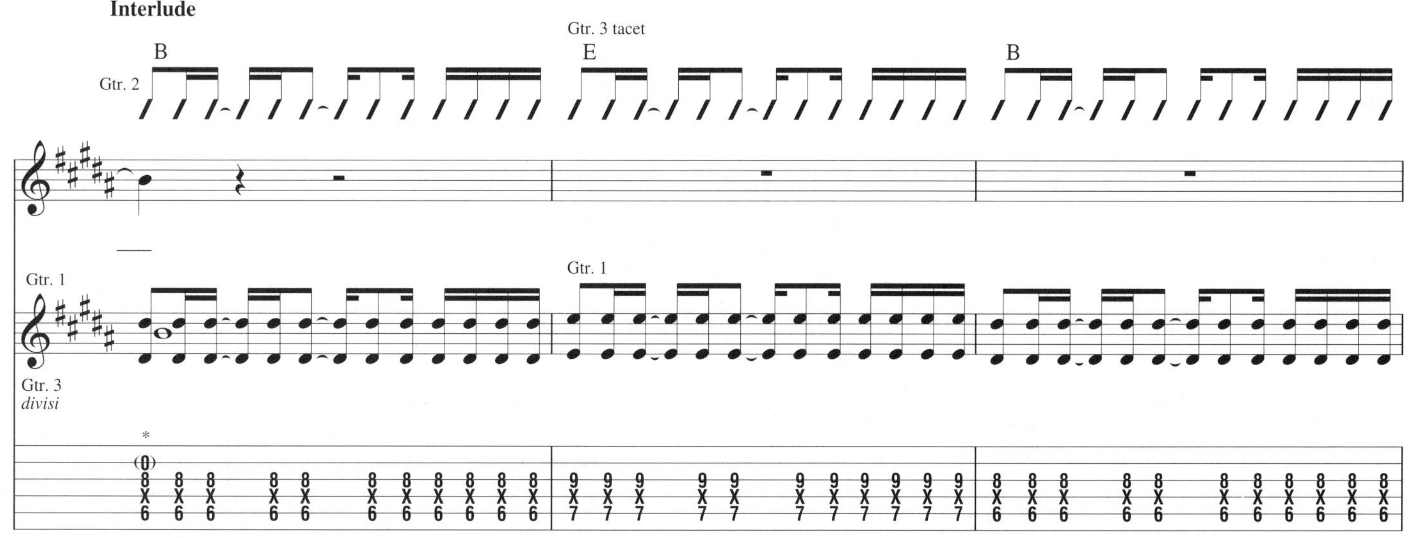
Interlude
Gtr. 3 tacet
B
E
B
Gtr. 2
Gtr. 1
Gtr. 3
divisi
*Tab for Gtr. 3 in parentheses.

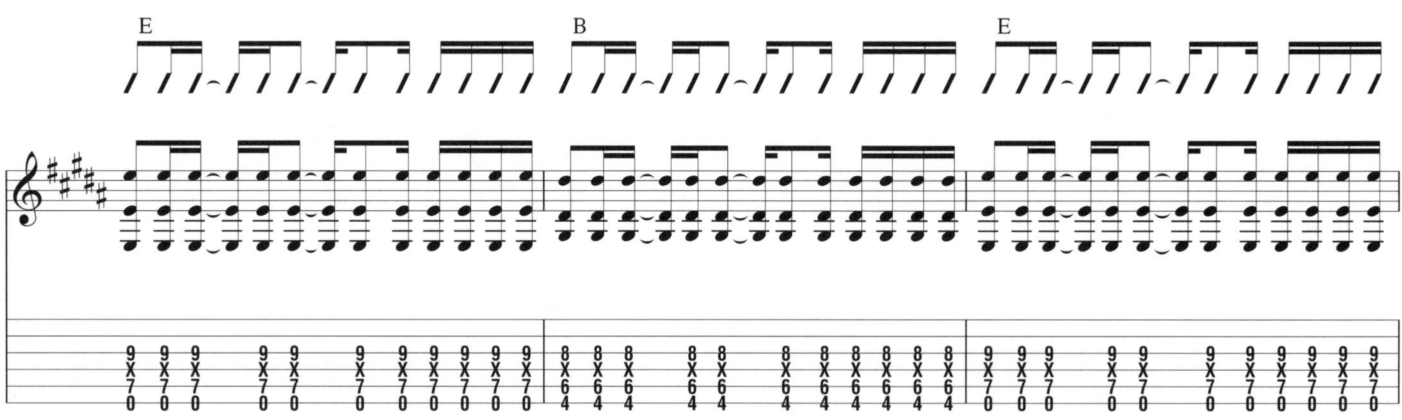
E
B
E

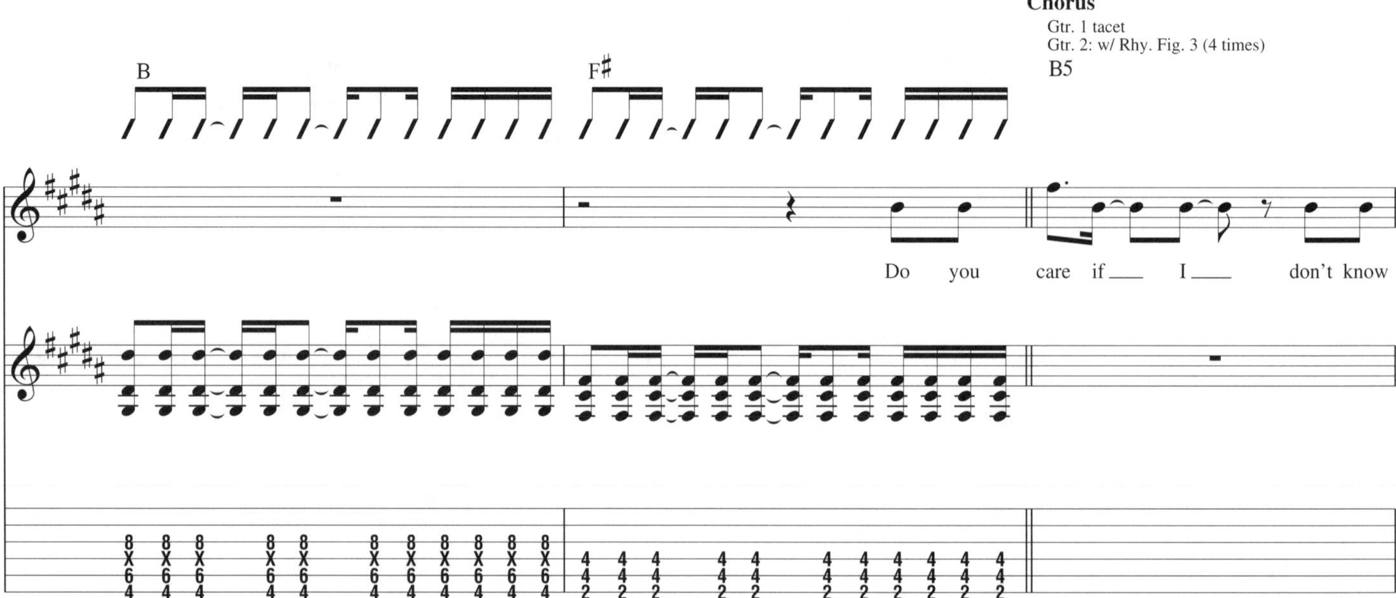
Chorus
Gtr. 1 tacet
Gtr. 2: w/ Rhy. Fig. 3 (4 times)
B
F♯
B5
Do you care if I don't know

F♯sus4
G♯m7
what to say? Will you sleep to - night, or will you

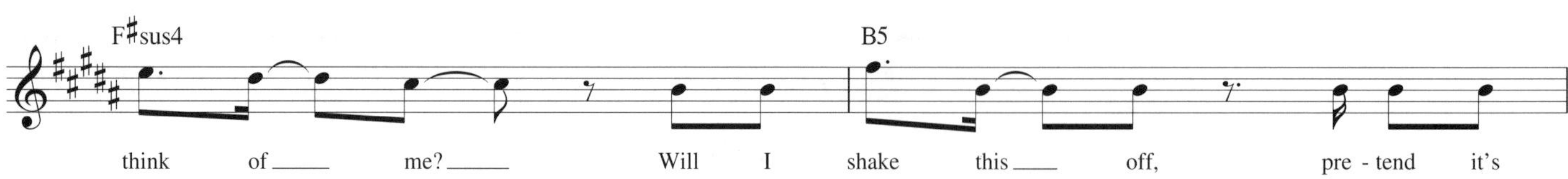
F♯sus4
B5
think of me? Will I shake this off, pre - tend it's

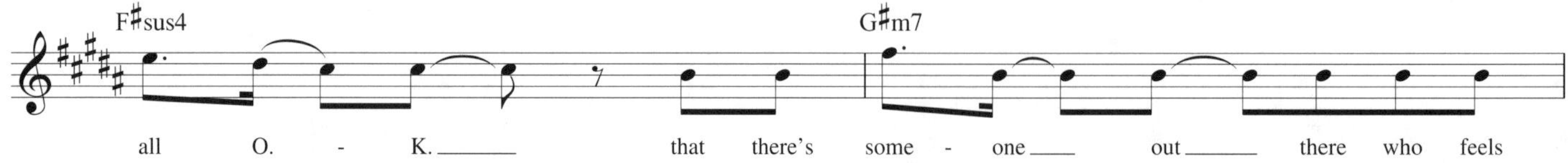
F♯sus4
G♯m7
all O. - K. that there's some - one out there who feels

*Tab for Gtr. 3 in parentheses.

The End With You

Words and Music by Tom De Longe and Travis Barker

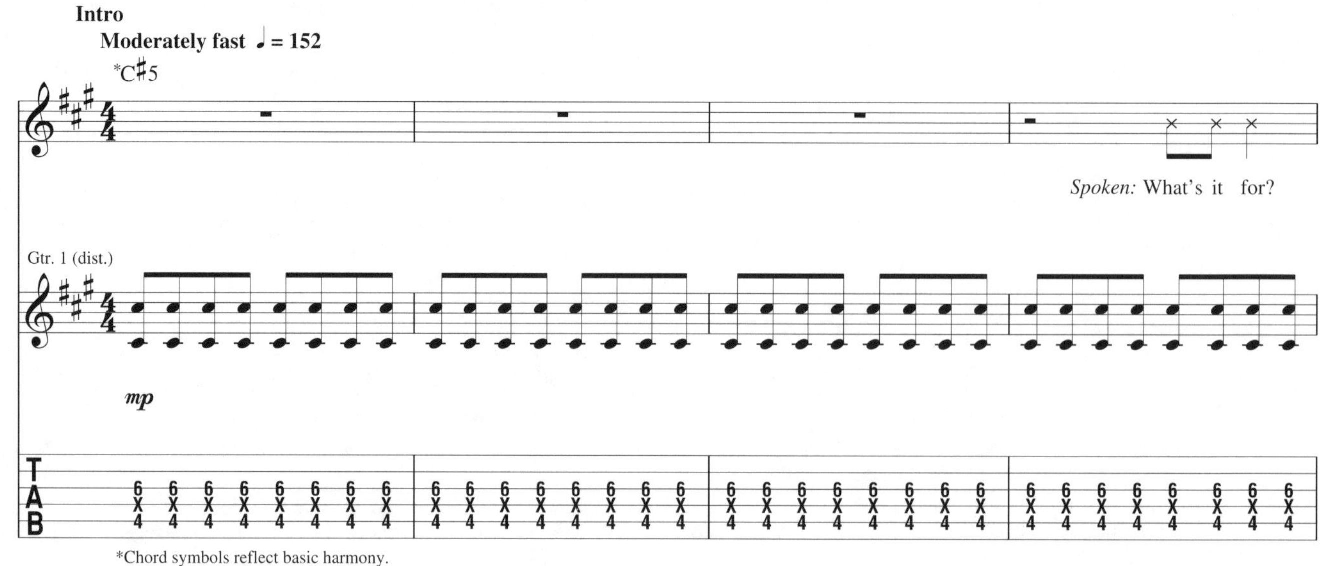

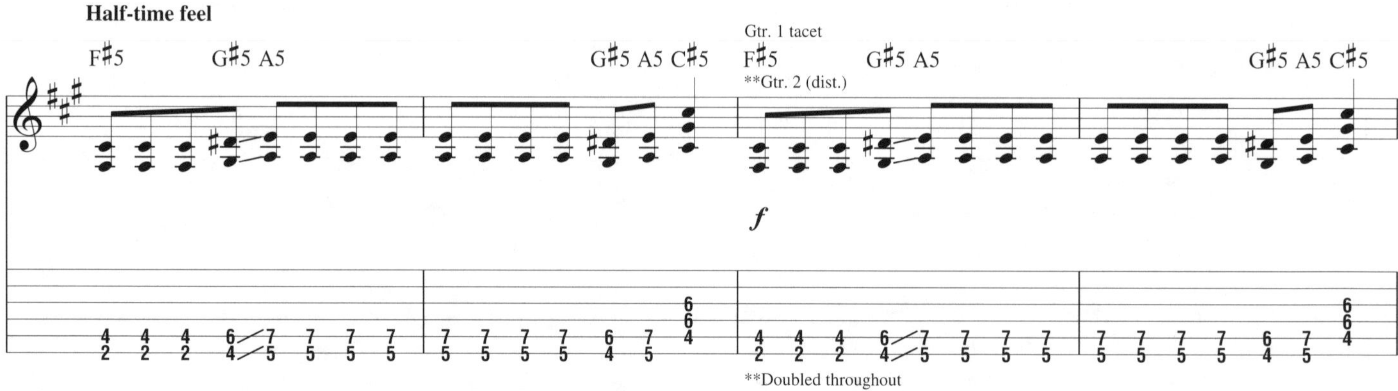

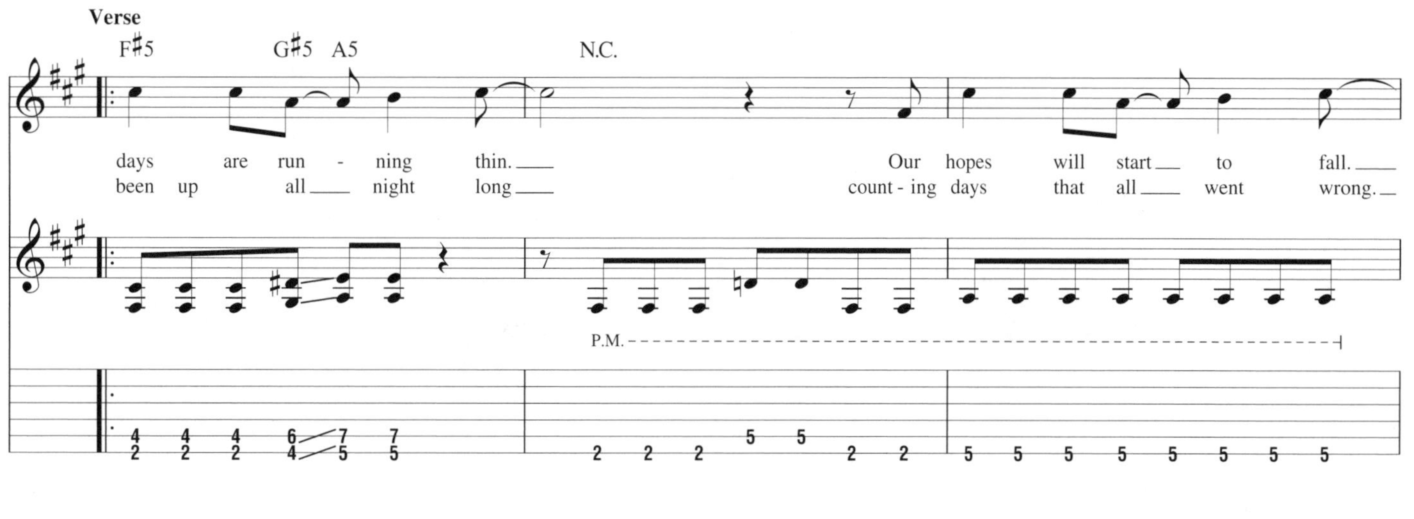
Verse
F♯5
G♯5 A5
N.C.
days are run - ning thin.___ Our hopes will start___ to fall.___
been up all___ night long___ count - ing days that all___ went wrong.___
P.M.

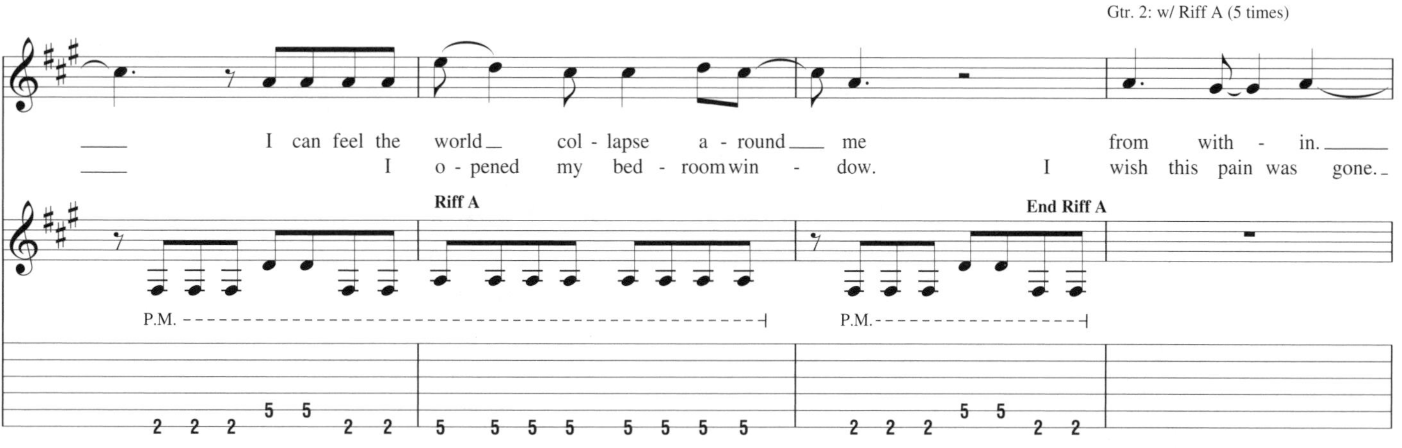
Gtr. 2: w/ Riff A (5 times)
___ I can feel the world___ col - lapse a - round___ me from with - in.___
___ I o - pened my bed - room win - dow. I wish this pain was gone.___
Riff A
End Riff A
P.M.
P.M.

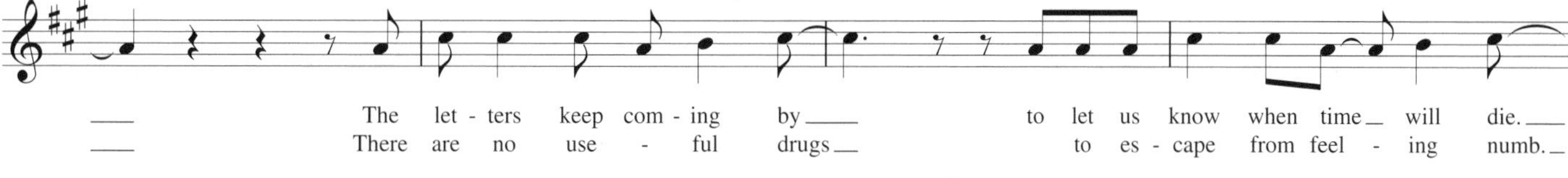
___ The let - ters keep com - ing by___ to let us know when time___ will die.___
___ There are no use - ful drugs___ to es - cape from feel - ing numb.___

___ And please, God, will you for - give___ us and give us one___ more try.___
___ I re - mem - ber___ an a - maz - ing birth - day. I re - mem - ber when I was young.___

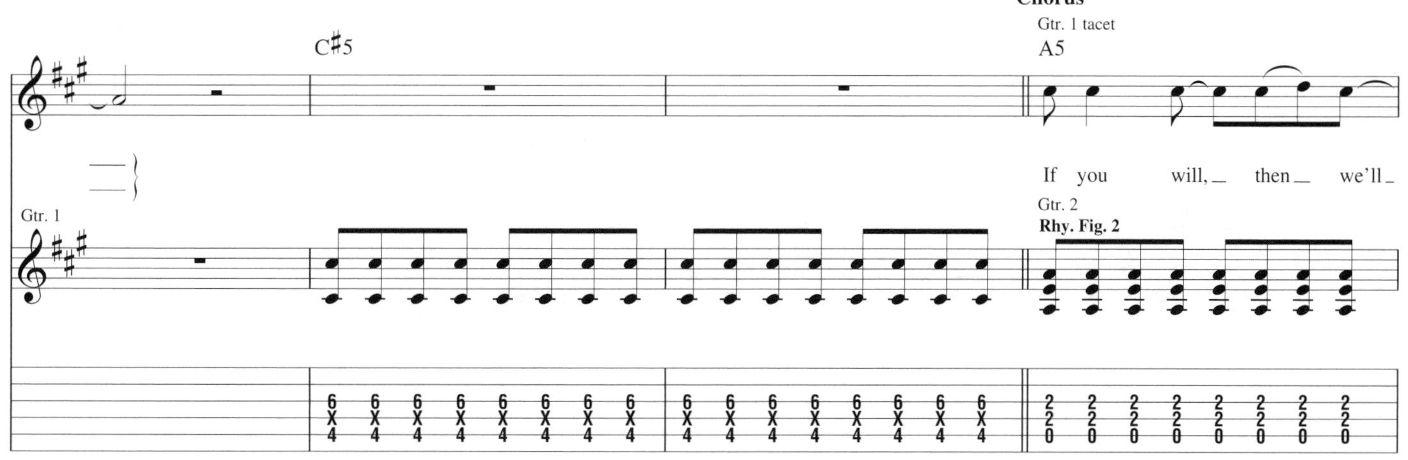
C♯5
Chorus
Gtr. 1 tacet
A5
If you will,___ then___ we'll___
Gtr. 1
Gtr. 2
Rhy. Fig. 2

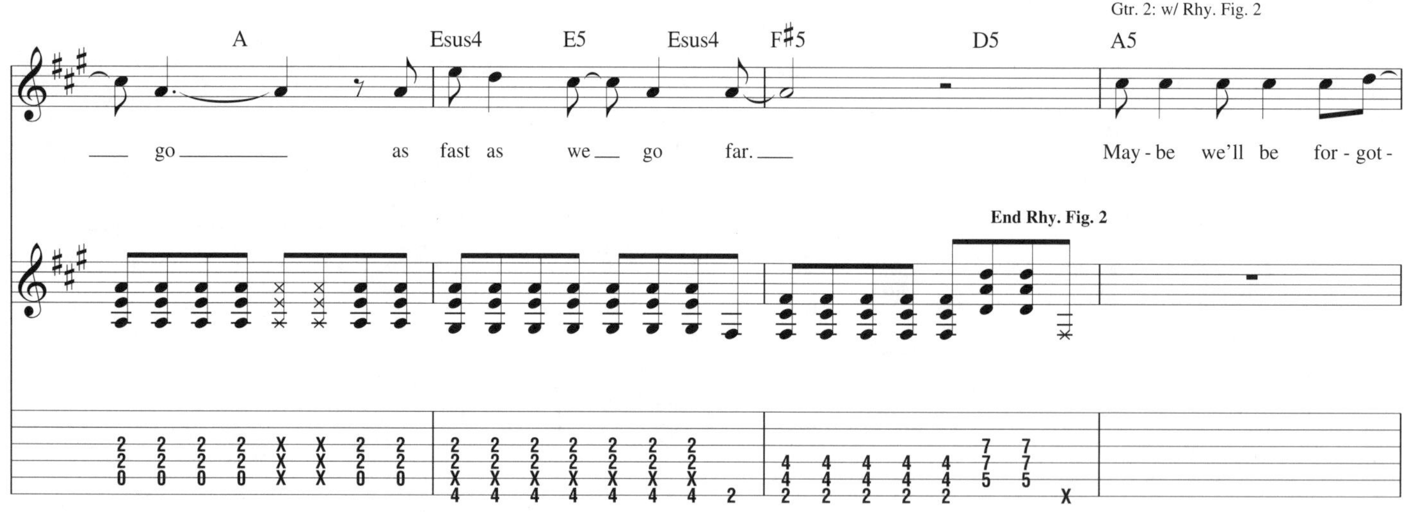

Gtr. 2: w/ Rhy. Fig. 2
A
Esus4
E5
Esus4
F♯5
D5
A5
go as fast as we go far.
May - be we'll be for - got -
End Rhy. Fig. 2

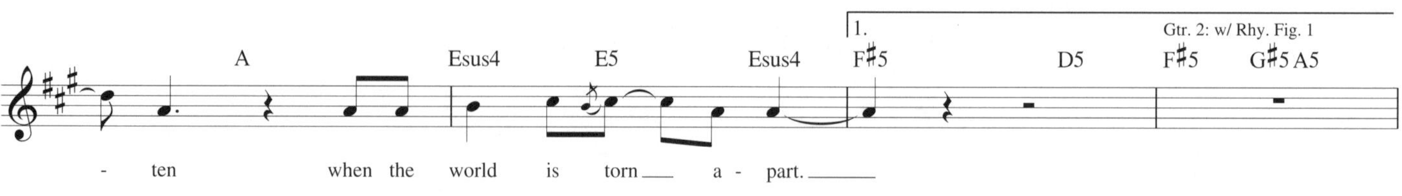

1.
Gtr. 2: w/ Rhy. Fig. 1
A
Esus4
E5
Esus4
F♯5
D5
F♯5
G♯5 A5
- ten when the world is torn a - part.

G♯5 A5 C♯5
F♯5
G♯5 A5
G♯5 A5 C♯5
2.
F♯5
D5
2. I've
'Cause the

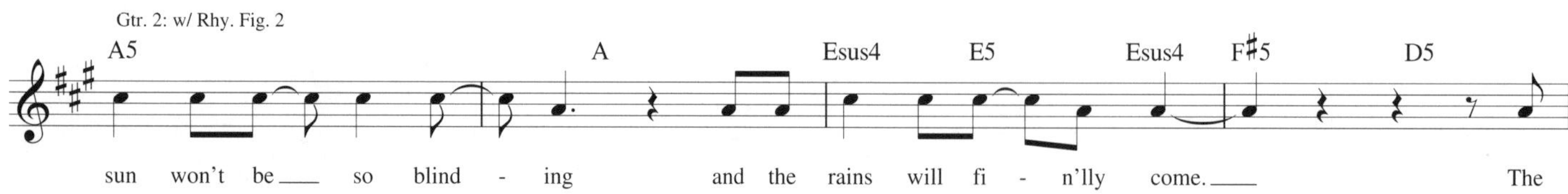

Gtr. 2: w/ Rhy. Fig. 2
A5
A
Esus4
E5
Esus4
F♯5
D5
sun won't be so blind - ing and the rains will fi - n'lly come. The

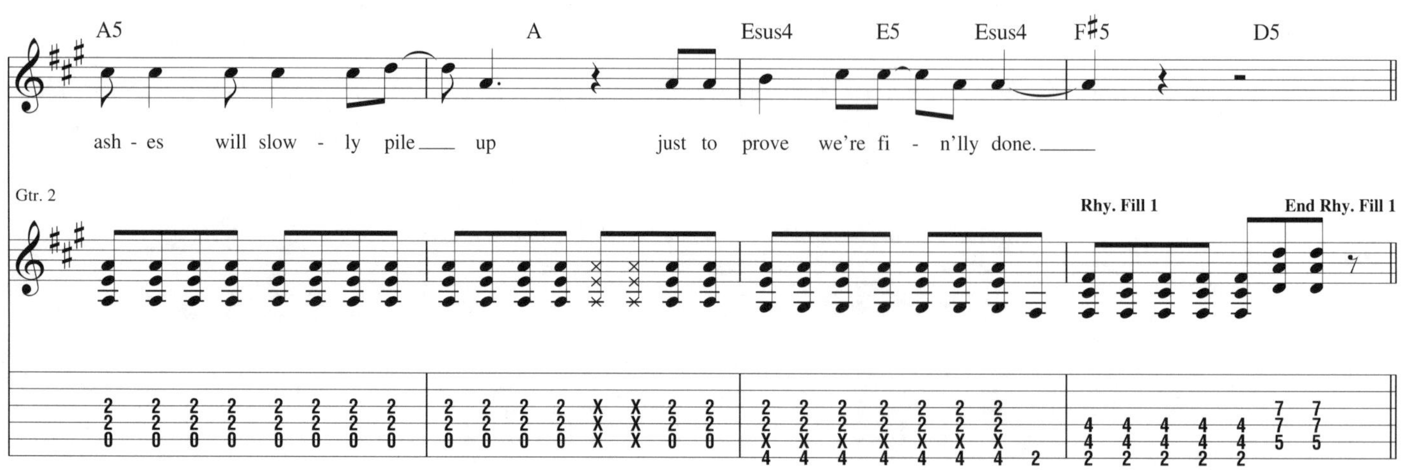

A5
A
Esus4
E5
Esus4
F♯5
D5
ash - es will slow - ly pile up just to prove we're fi - n'lly done.
Gtr. 2
Rhy. Fill 1
End Rhy. Fill 1

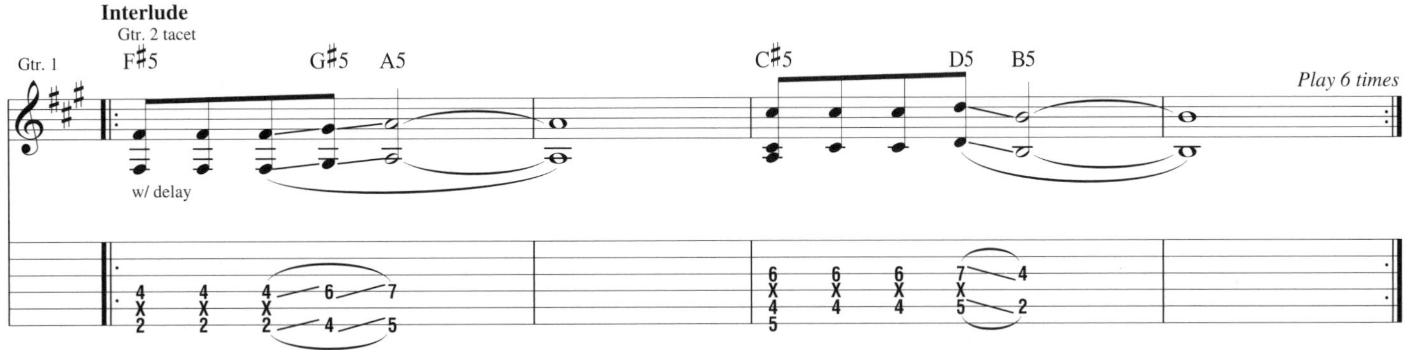
Interlude
Gtr. 2 tacet
Gtr. 1
F♯5 G♯5 A5 C♯5 D5 B5
Play 6 times
w/ delay

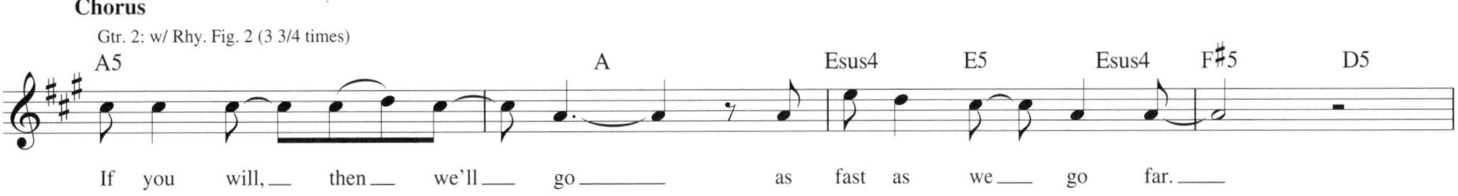
Chorus
Gtr. 2: w/ Rhy. Fig. 2 (3 3/4 times)
A5 A Esus4 E5 Esus4 F♯5 D5
If you will, then we'll go as fast as we go far.

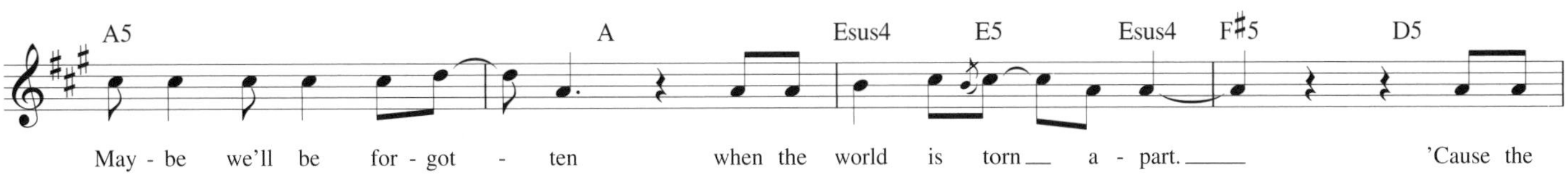
A5 A Esus4 E5 Esus4 F♯5 D5
May - be we'll be for - got - ten when the world is torn a - part. 'Cause the

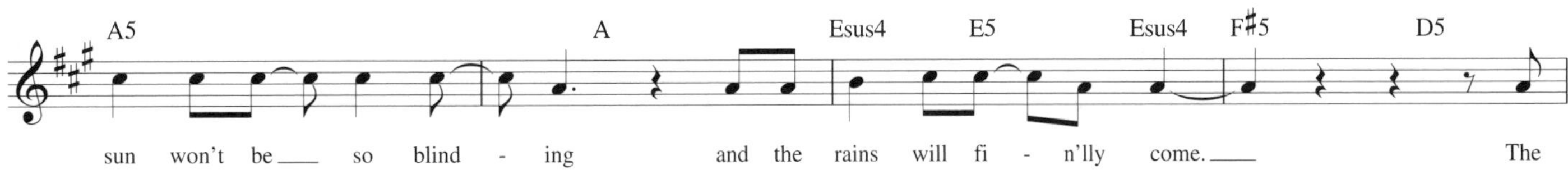
A5 A Esus4 E5 Esus4 F♯5 D5
sun won't be so blind - ing and the rains will fi - n'lly come. The

Gtr. 2: w/ Rhy. Fill 1
A5 A Esus4 E5 Esus4 F♯5 D5
ax - is will slow - ly pile up just to prove we're fi - n'lly done.

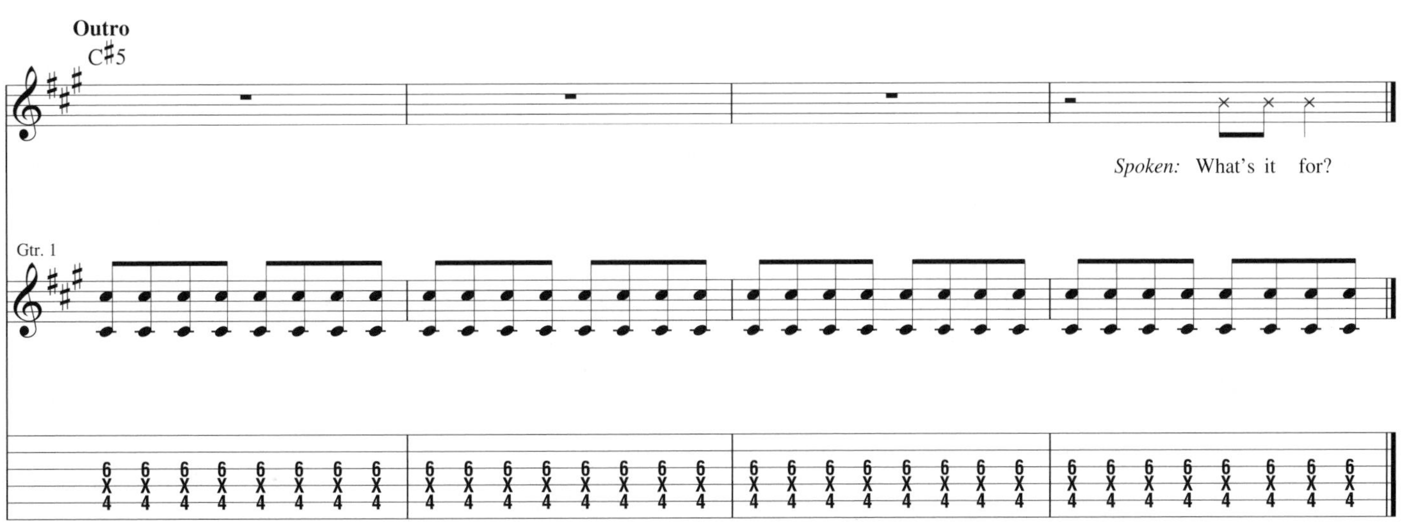
Outro
C♯5
Spoken: What's it for?
Gtr. 1

Elevator

Words and Music by Tom De Longe and Travis Barker

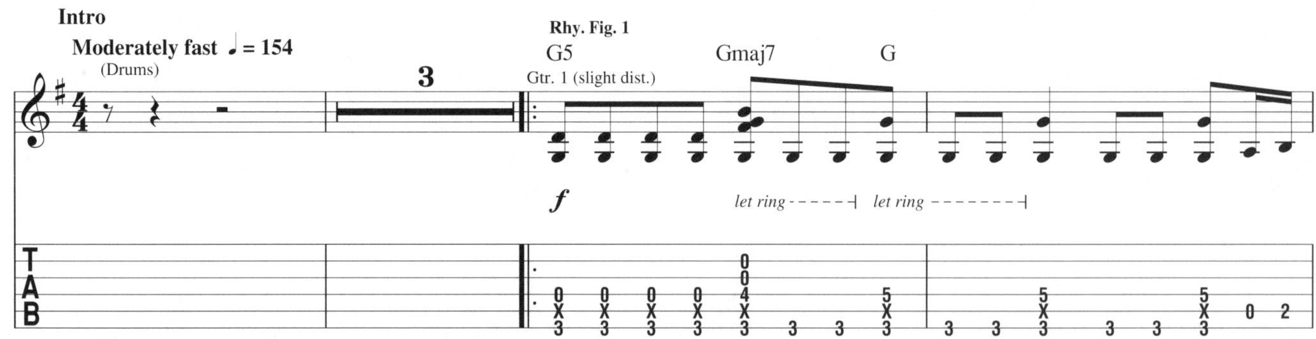

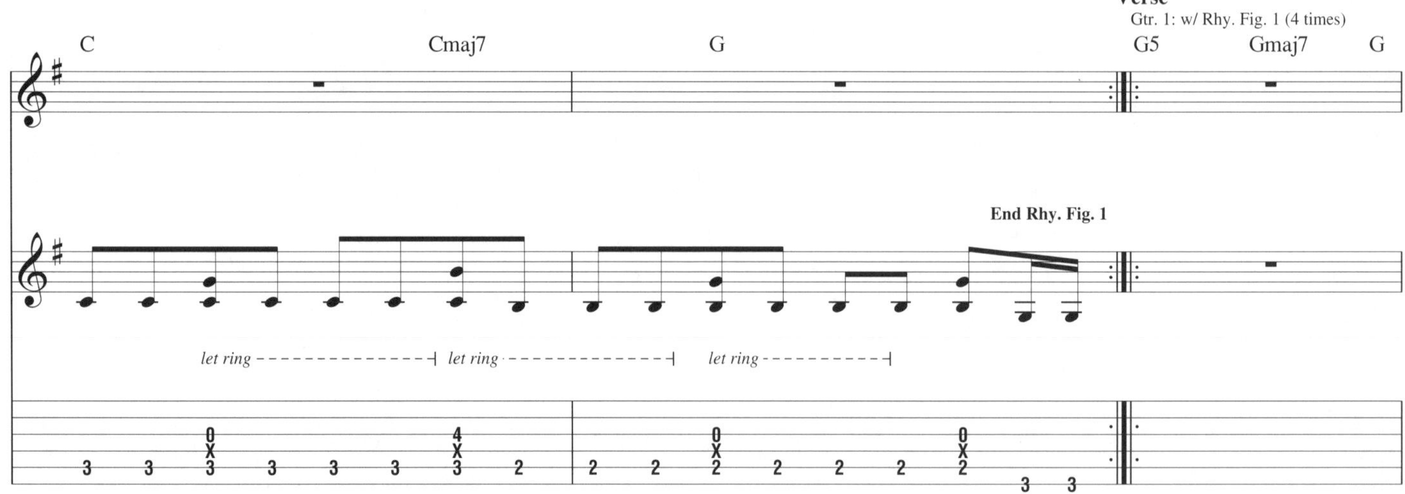

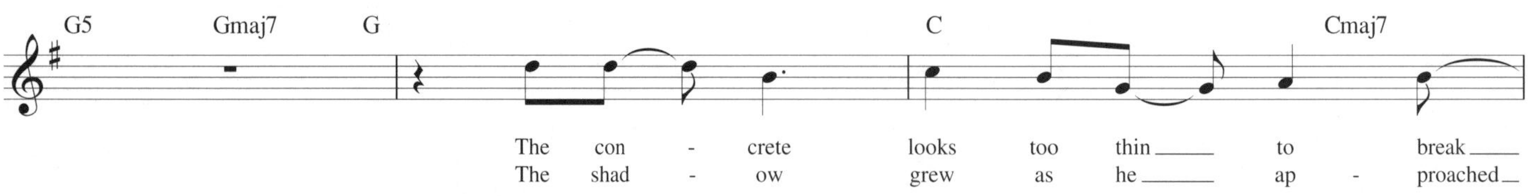

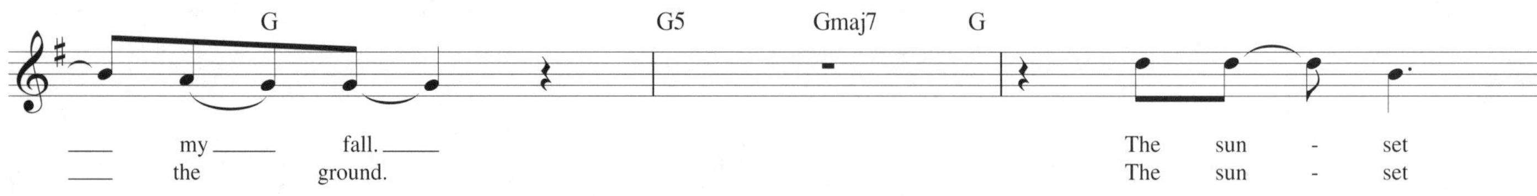

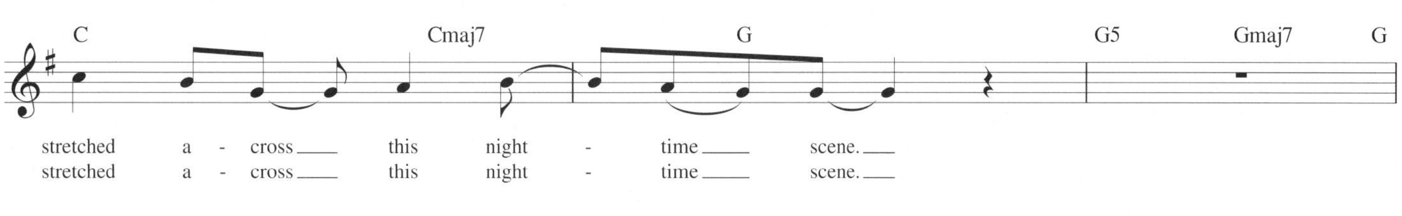
C
Cmaj7
G
G5
Gmaj7
G
stretched a - cross this night - time scene.
stretched a - cross this night - time scene.

C
Cmaj7
G
I count - ed peo - ple as I neared the street be - low.
They turned a - way as he came near the street be - low.

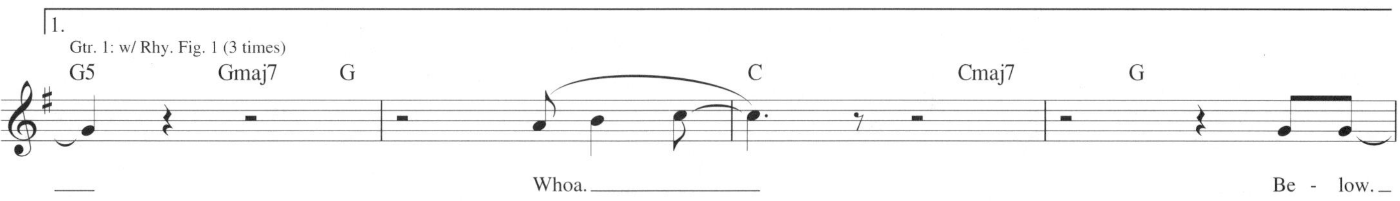
1.
Gtr. 1: w/ Rhy. Fig. 1 (3 times)
G5
Gmaj7
G
C
Cmaj7
G
Whoa.
Be - low.

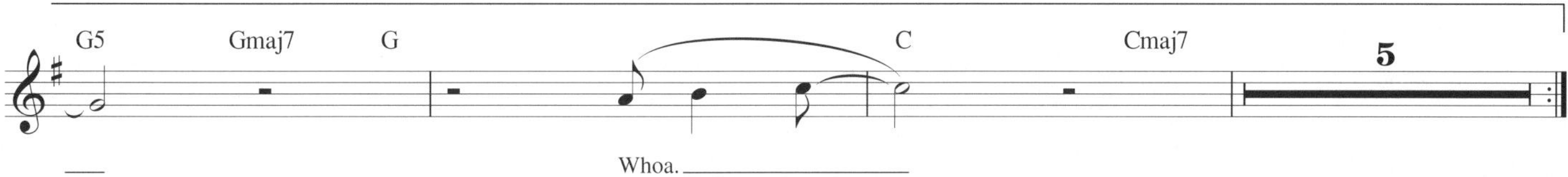
G5
Gmaj7
G
C
Cmaj7
5
Whoa.

2.
G
Gmaj7
G5
C
Cmaj7
Whoa.
Gtr. 1
Rhy. Fig. 2
let ring
let ring
let ring

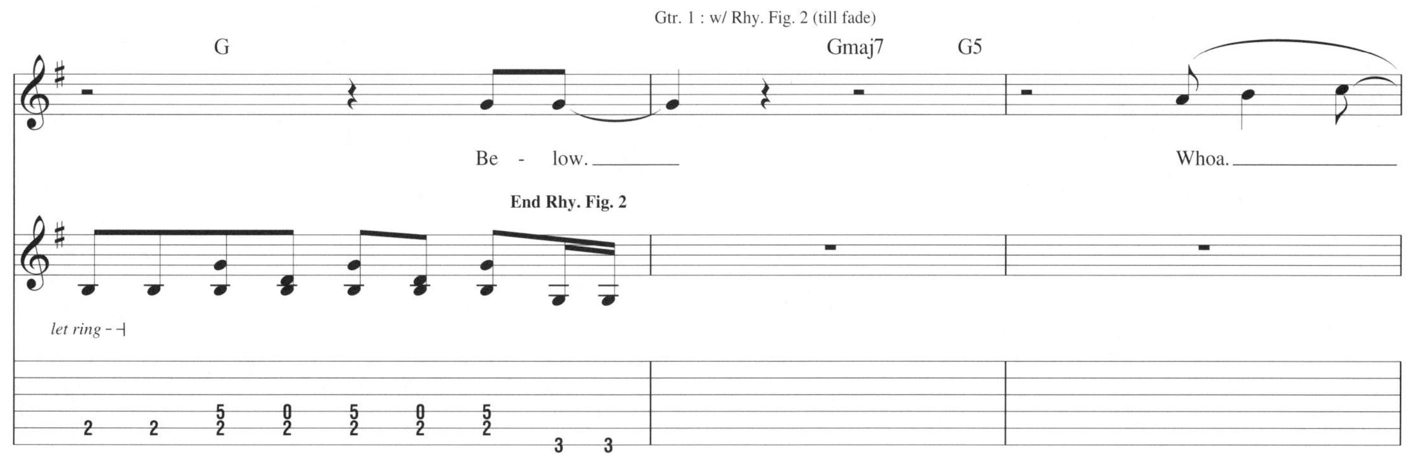
Gtr. 1 : w/ Rhy. Fig. 2 (till fade)
G
Gmaj7
G5
Be - low.
Whoa.
End Rhy. Fig. 2
let ring

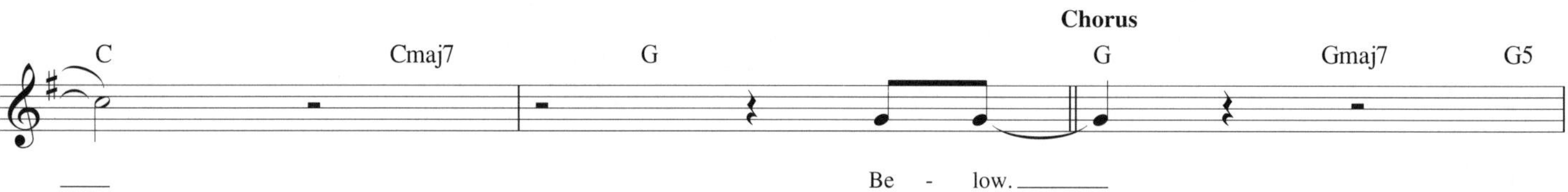
Chorus
C
Cmaj7
G
G
Gmaj7
G5
Be - low.

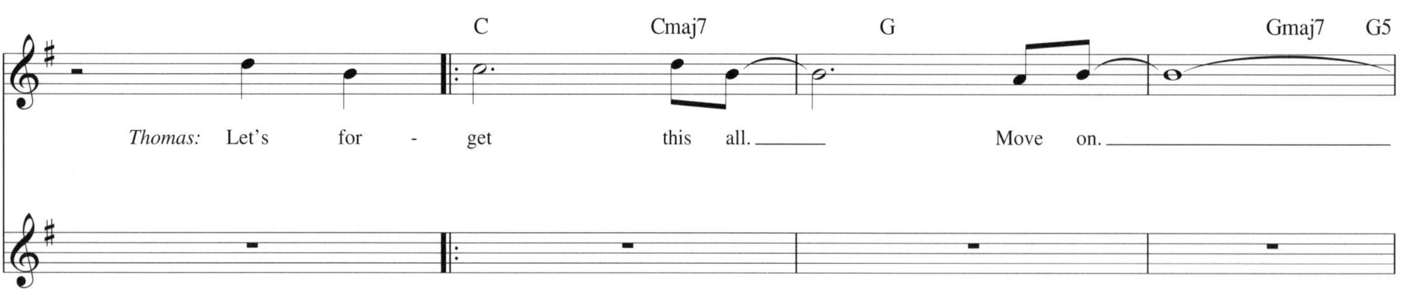
C
Cmaj7
G
Gmaj7
G5
Thomas: Let's for - get this all. Move on.

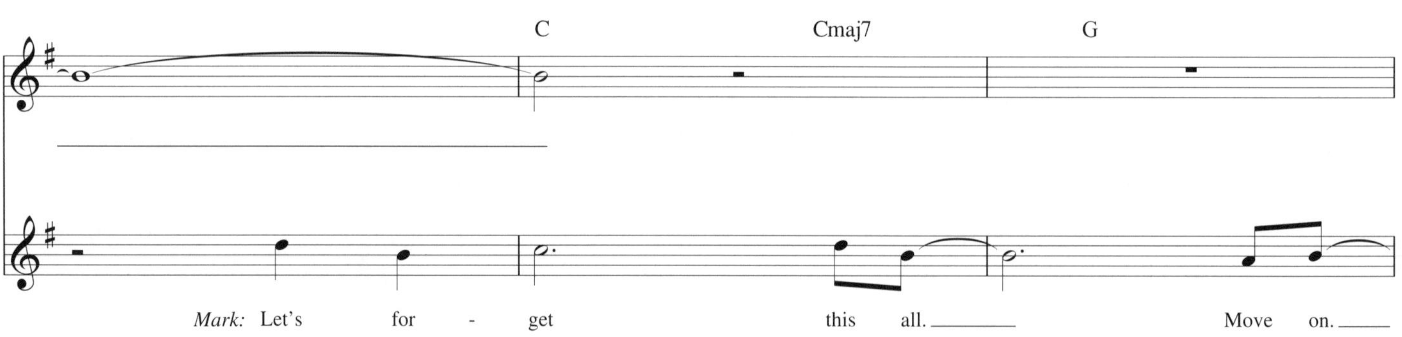
C
Cmaj7
G
Mark: Let's for - get this all. Move on.

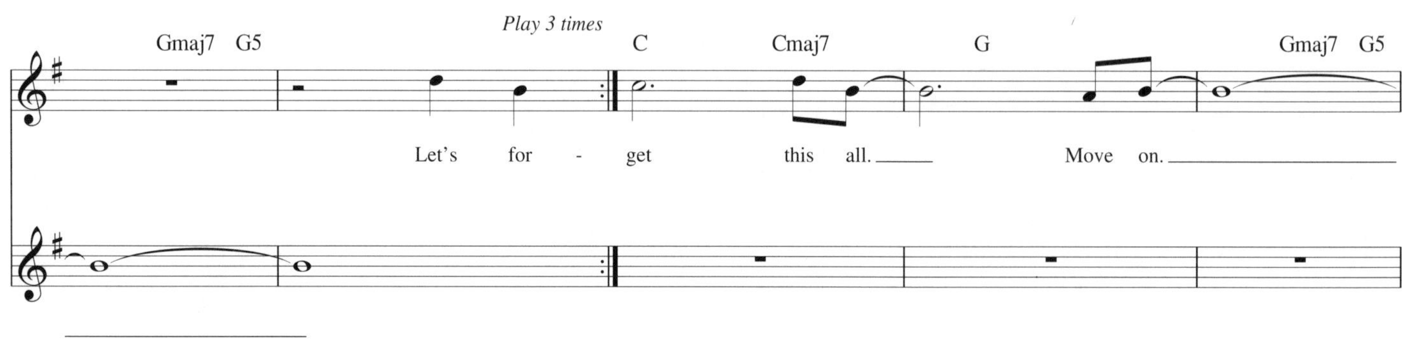
Play 3 times
Gmaj7
G5
C
Cmaj7
G
Gmaj7
G5
Let's for - get this all. Move on.

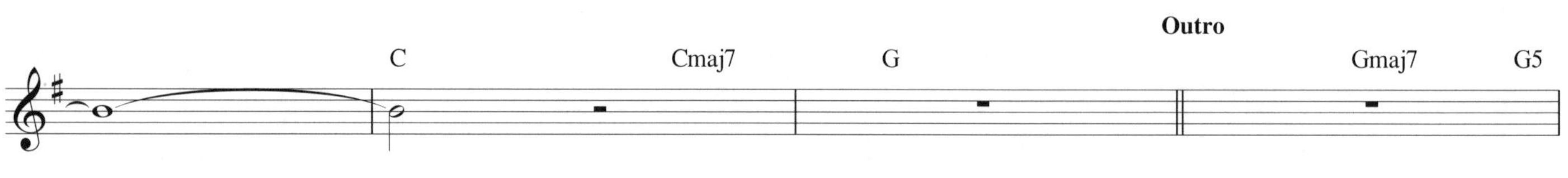
Outro
C
Cmaj7
G
Gmaj7
G5

Begin fade
Fade out
C
Cmaj7
G
Gmaj7 G5
C
Cmaj7
G
Gmaj7
G5

Instrumental

By Tom De Longe and Travis Barker

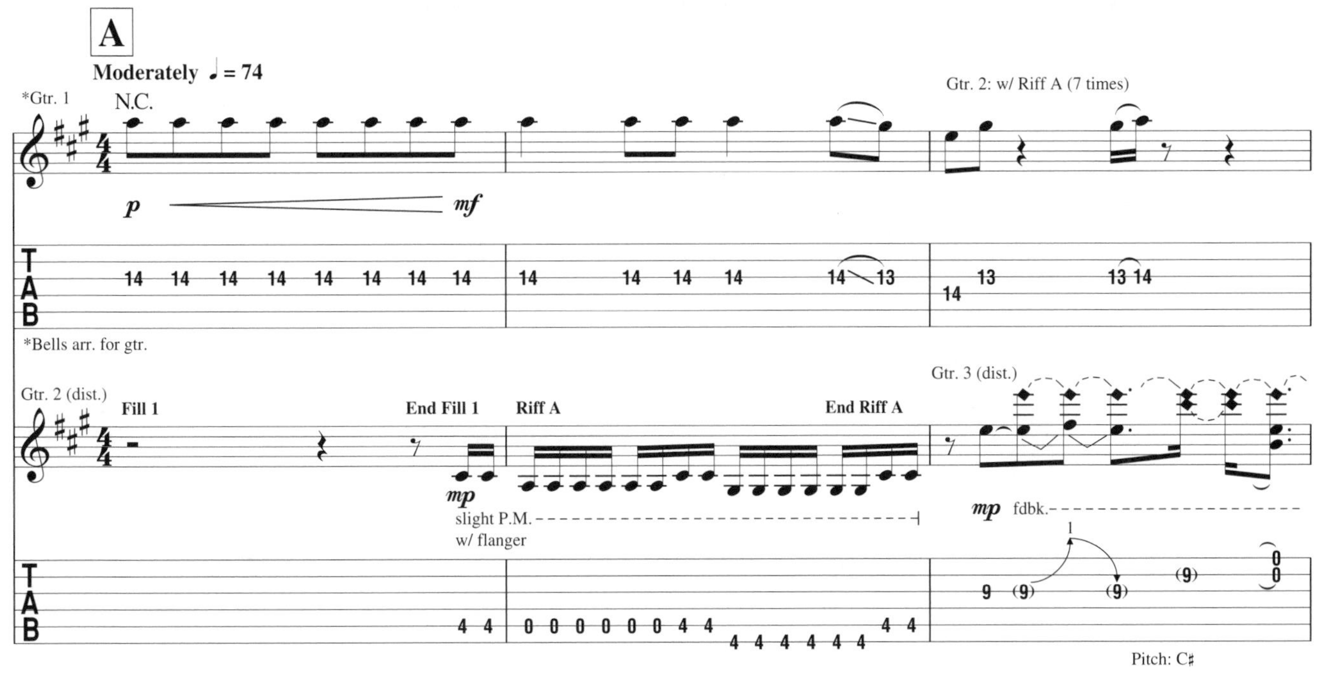

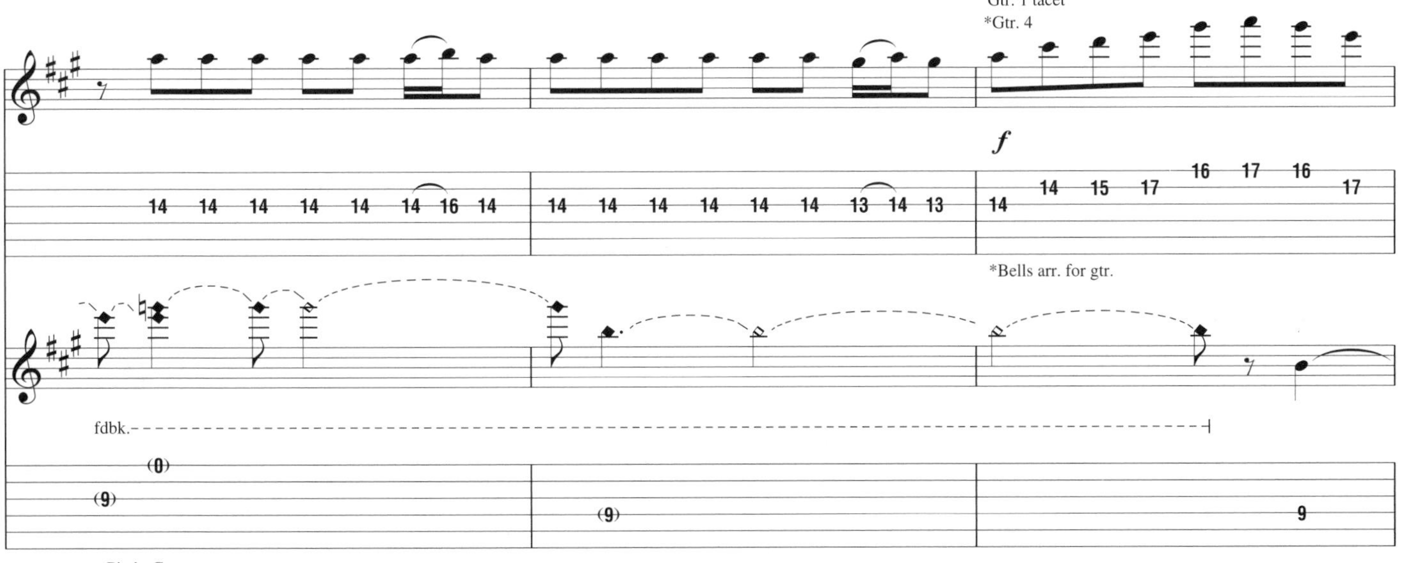

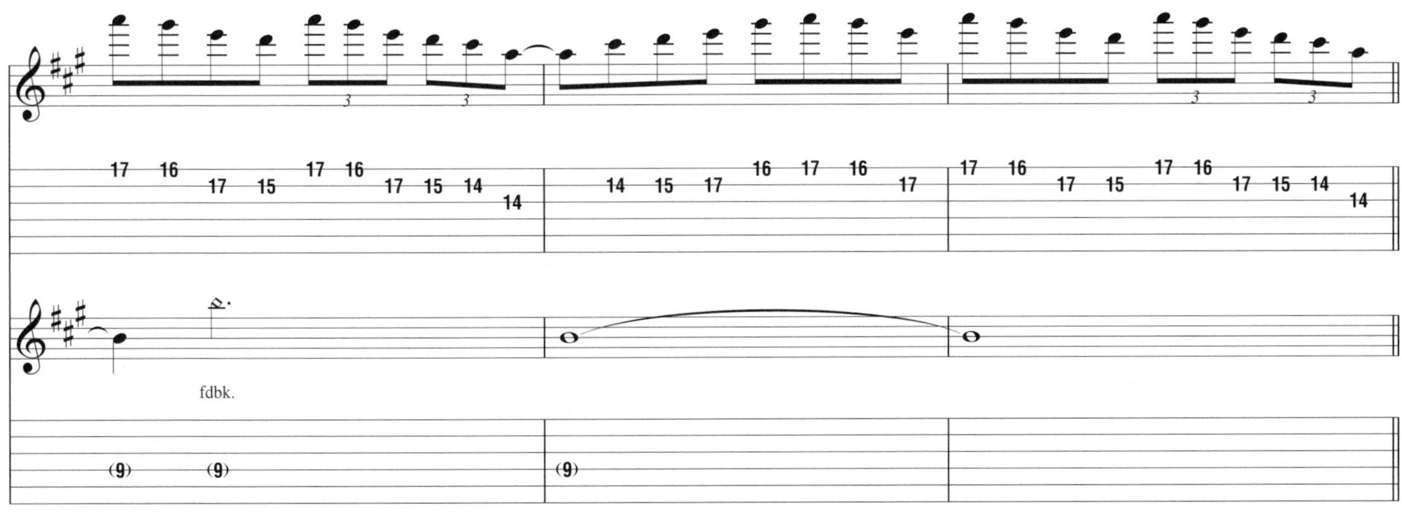

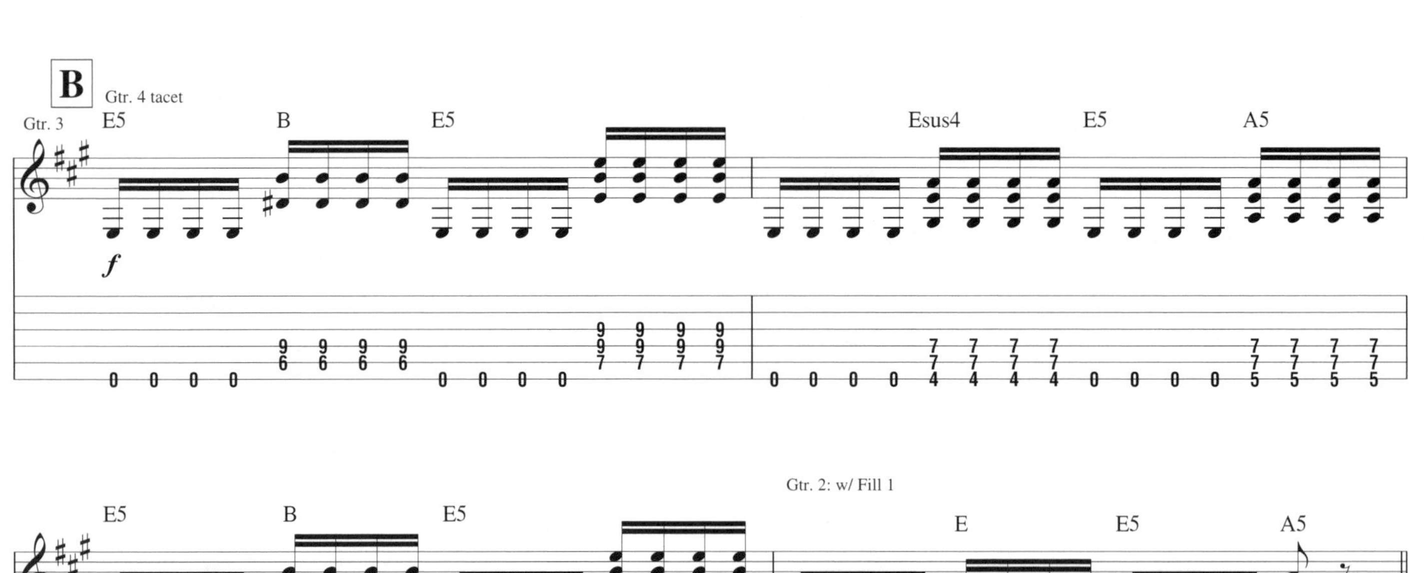
B
Gtr. 4 tacet
Gtr. 3
E5
B
E5
Esus4
E5
A5
f

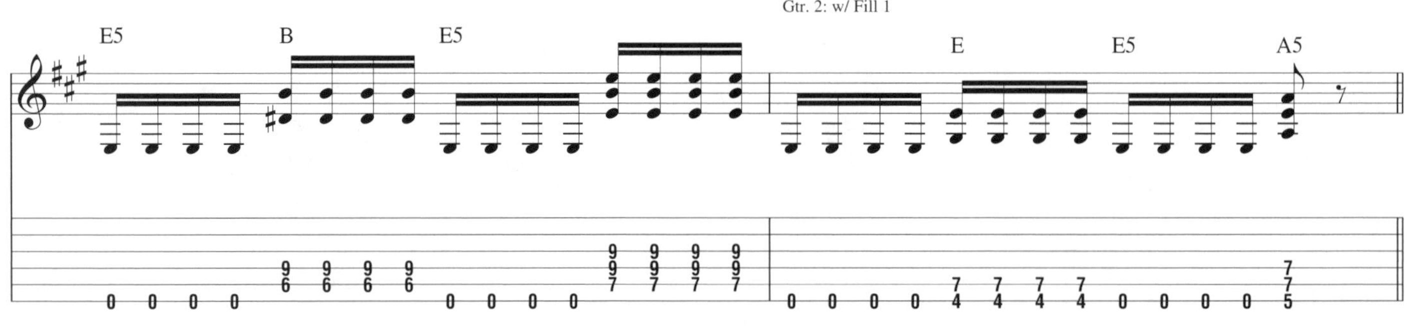
Gtr. 2: w/ Fill 1
E5
B
E5
E
E5
A5

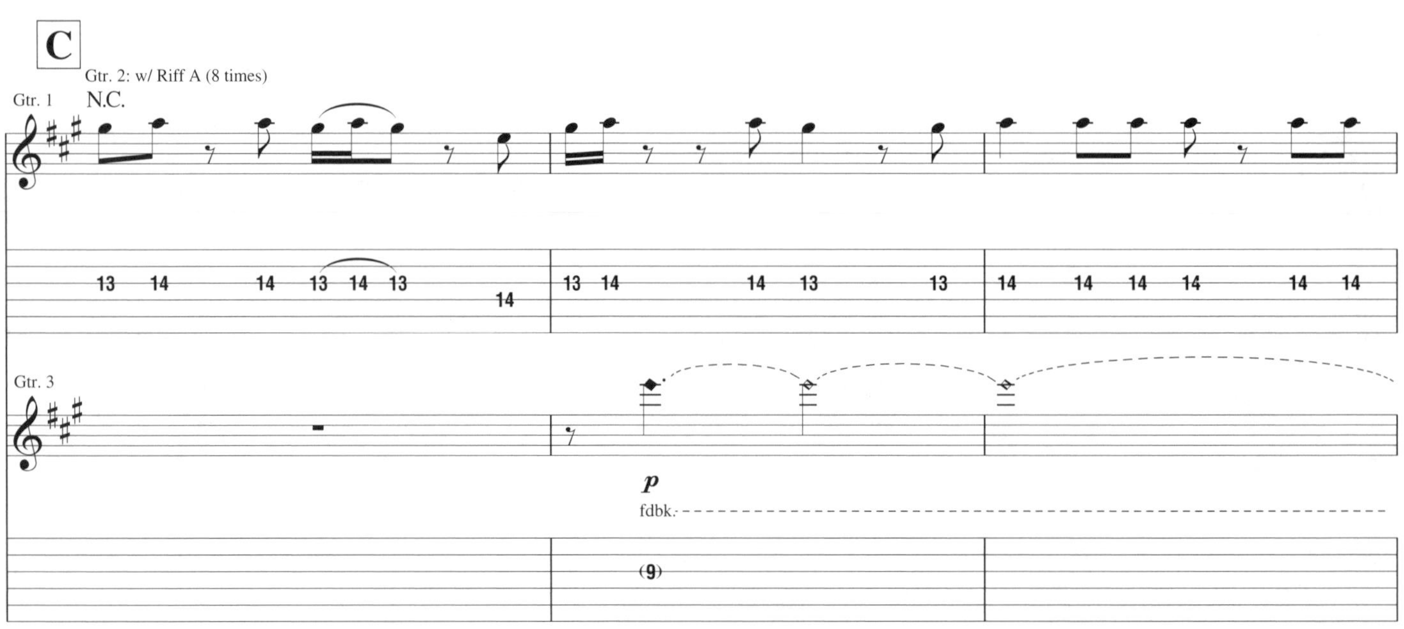
C
Gtr. 2: w/ Riff A (8 times)
Gtr. 1
N.C.
Gtr. 3
p
fdbk.

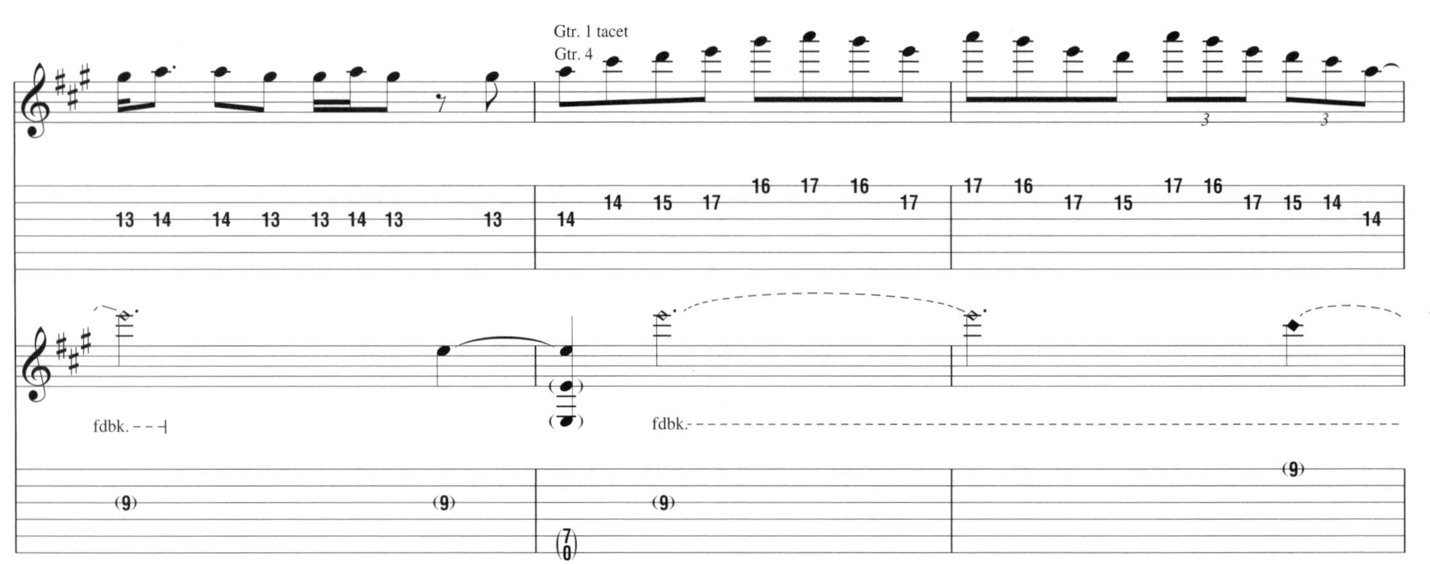
Gtr. 1 tacet
Gtr. 4
fdbk.
fdbk.

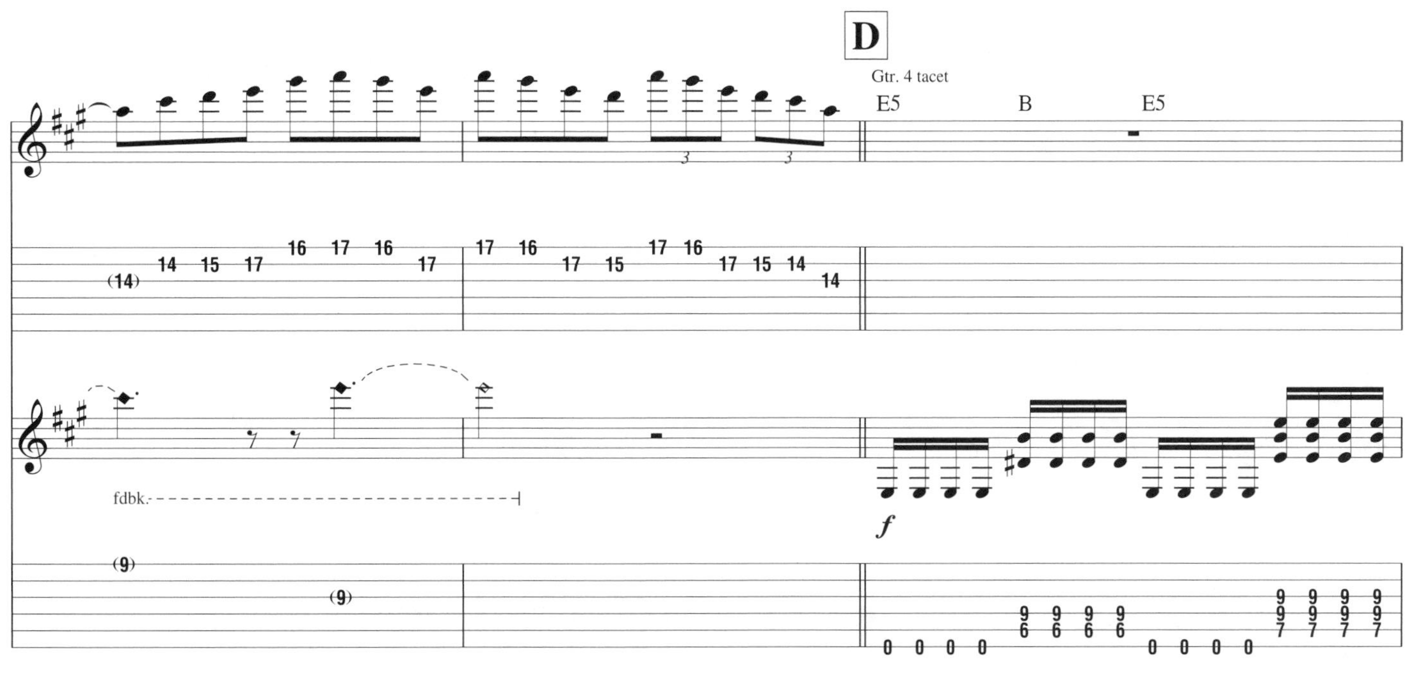
D
Gtr. 4 tacet
E5
B
E5
fdbk.

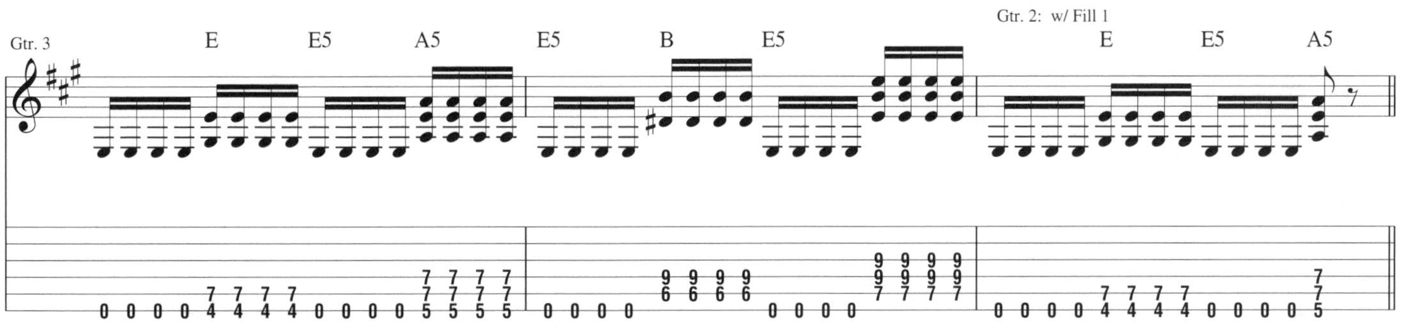
Gtr. 3
E
E5
A5
E5
B
E5
Gtr. 2: w/ Fill 1
E
E5
A5

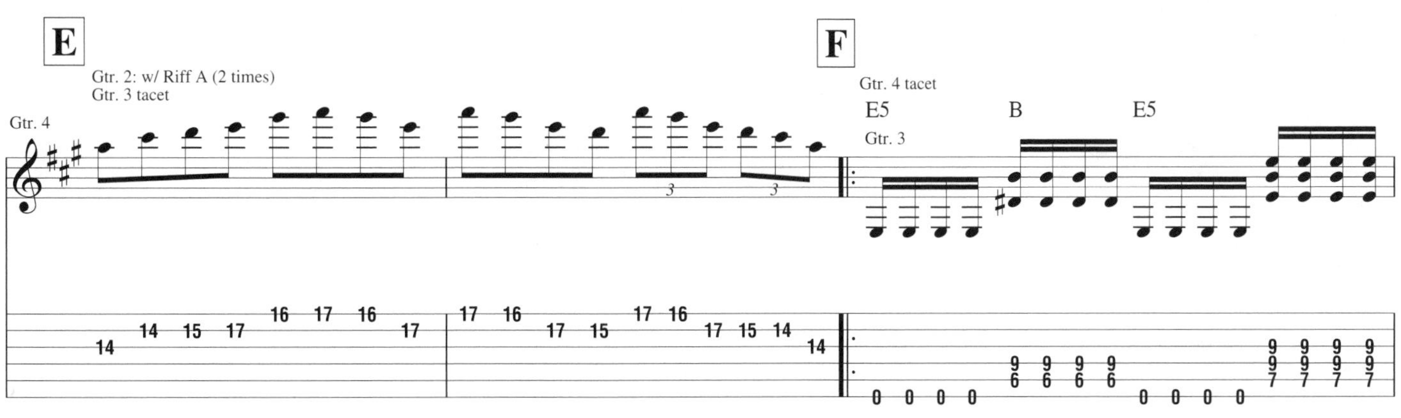
E
Gtr. 2: w/ Riff A (2 times)
Gtr. 3 tacet
Gtr. 4
F
Gtr. 4 tacet
E5
B
E5
Gtr. 3

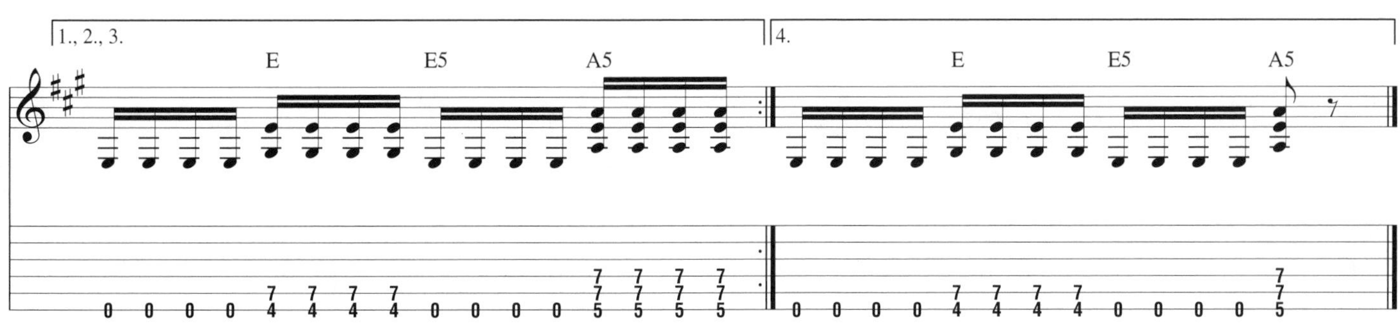
1., 2., 3.
E
E5
A5
4.
E
E5
A5

Guitar Notation Legend

Guitar Music can be notated three different ways: on a *musical staff*, in *tablature*, and in *rhythm slashes*.

RHYTHM SLASHES are written above the staff. Strum chords in the rhythm indicated. Use the chord diagrams found at the top of the first page of the transcription for the appropriate chord voicings. Round noteheads indicate single notes.

THE MUSICAL STAFF shows pitches and rhythms and is divided by bar lines into measures. Pitches are named after the first seven letters of the alphabet.

TABLATURE graphically represents the guitar fingerboard. Each horizontal line represents a a string, and each number represents a fret.

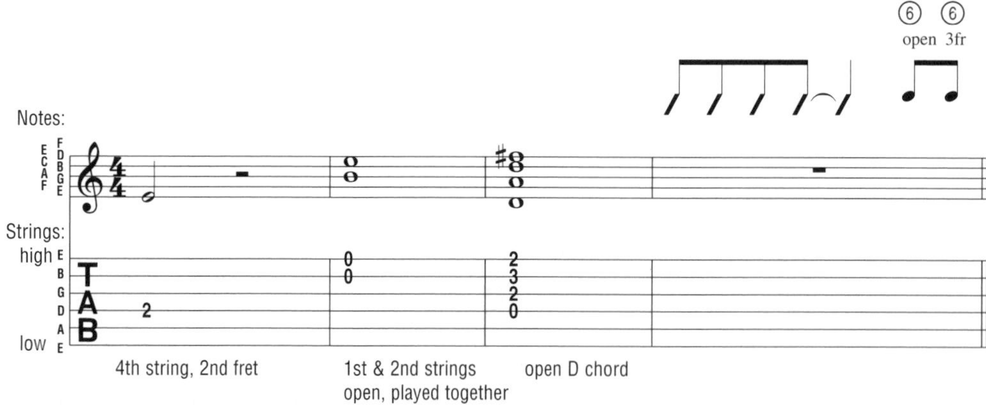

Definitions for Special Guitar Notation

HALF-STEP BEND: Strike the note and bend up 1/2 step.

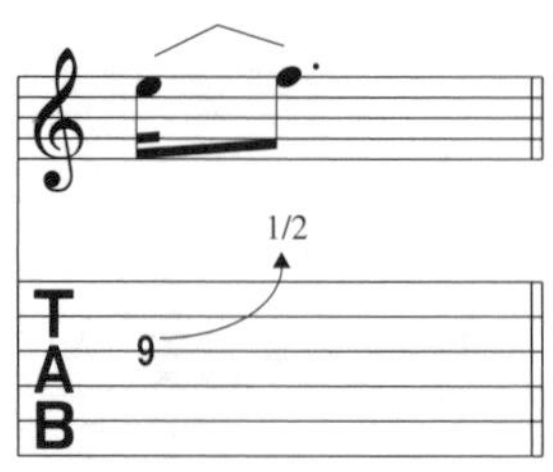

WHOLE-STEP BEND: Strike the note and bend up one step.

GRACE NOTE BEND: Strike the note and immediately bend up as indicated.

SLIGHT (MICROTONE) BEND: Strike the note and bend up 1/4 step.

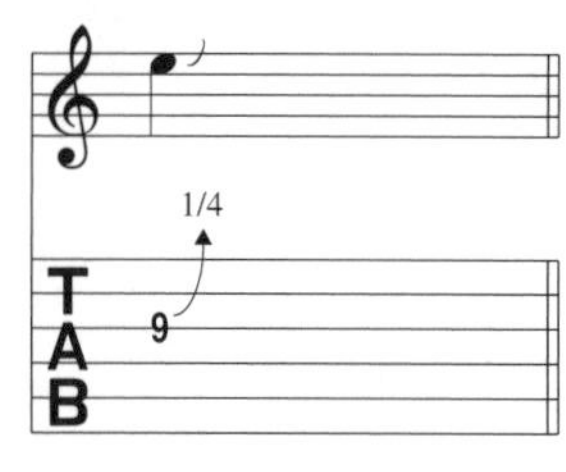

BEND AND RELEASE: Strike the note and bend up as indicated, then release back to the original note. Only the first note is struck.

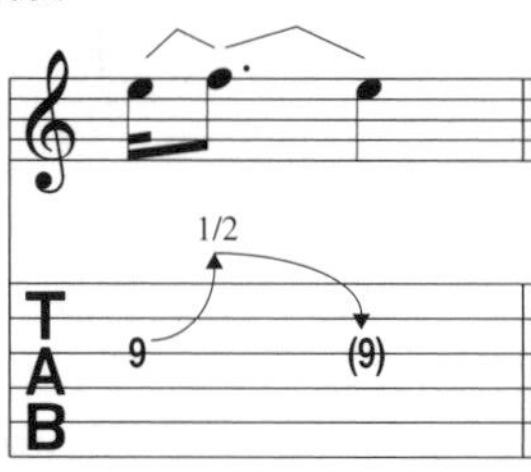

PRE-BEND: Bend the note as indicated, then strike it.

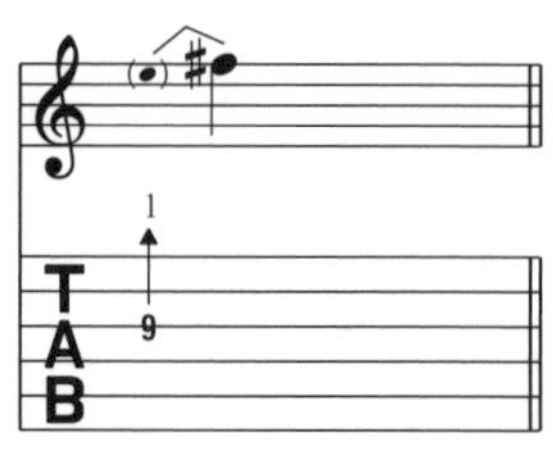

PRE-BEND AND RELEASE: Bend the note as indicated. Strike it and release the bend back to the original note.

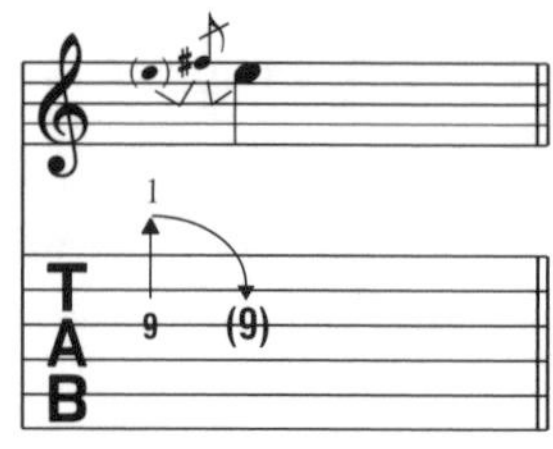

UNISON BEND: Strike the two notes simultaneously and bend the lower note up to the pitch of the higher.

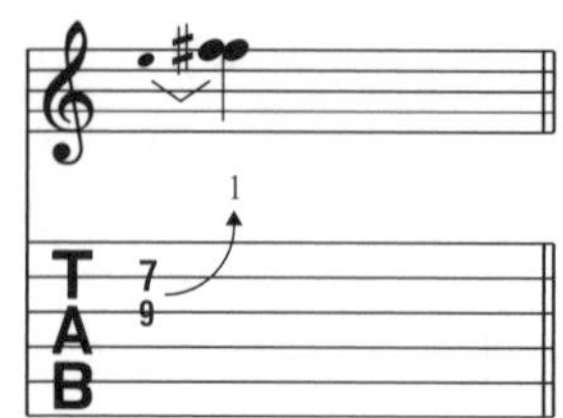

VIBRATO: The string is vibrated by rapidly bending and releasing the note with the fretting hand.

WIDE VIBRATO: The pitch is varied to a greater degree by vibrating with the fretting hand.

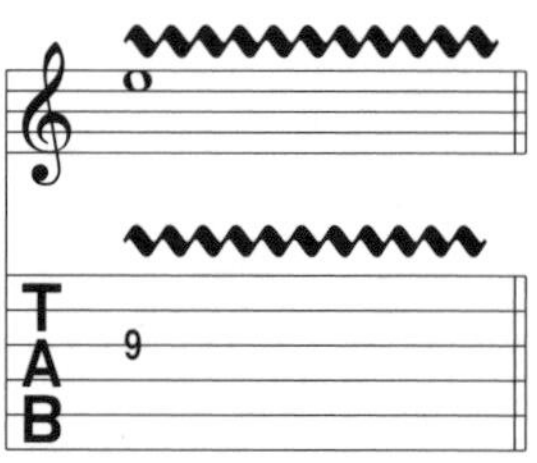

HAMMER-ON: Strike the first (lower) note with one finger, then sound the higher note (on the same string) with another finger by fretting it without picking.

PULL-OFF: Place both fingers on the notes to be sounded. Strike the first note and without picking, pull the finger off to sound the second (lower) note.

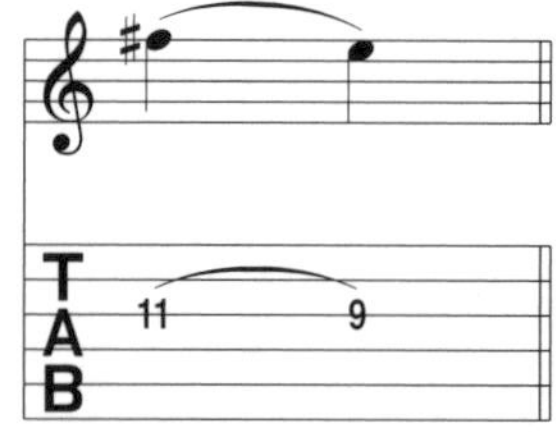

LEGATO SLIDE: Strike the first note and then slide the same fret-hand finger up or down to the second note. The second note is not struck.

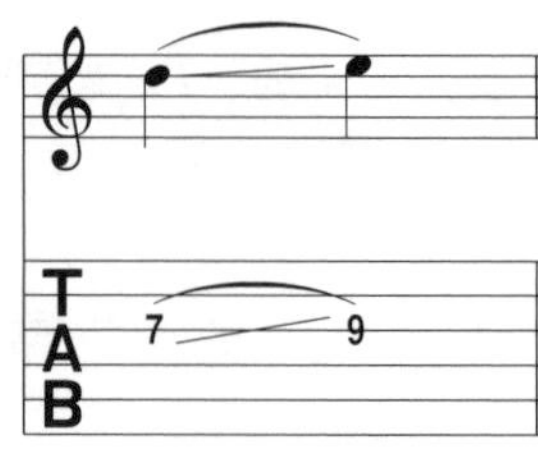

SHIFT SLIDE: Same as legato slide, except the second note is struck.

TRILL: Very rapidly alternate between the notes indicated by continuously hammering on and pulling off.

TAPPING: Hammer ("tap") the fret indicated with the pick-hand index or middle finger and pull off to the note fretted by the fret hand.

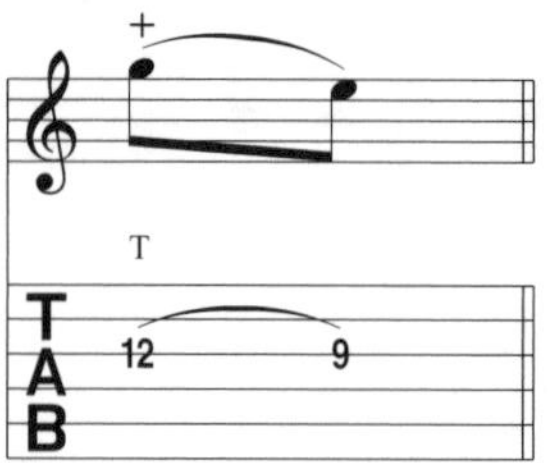

NATURAL HARMONIC: Strike the note while the fret-hand lightly touches the string directly over the fret indicated.

PINCH HARMONIC: The note is fretted normally and a harmonic is produced by adding the edge of the thumb or the tip of the index finger of the pick hand to the normal pick attack.

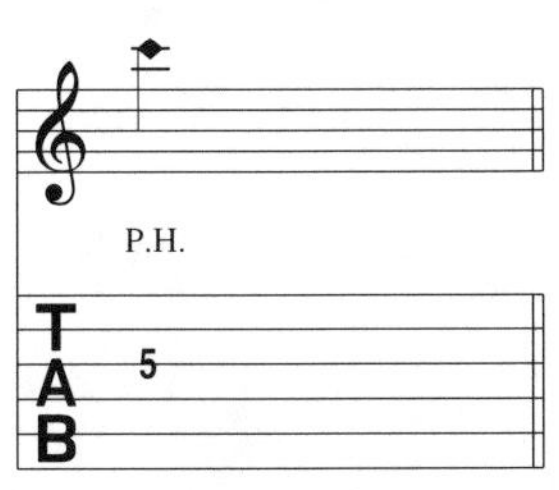

HARP HARMONIC: The note is fretted normally and a harmonic is produced by gently resting the pick hand's index finger directly above the indicated fret (in parentheses) while the pick hand's thumb or pick assists by plucking the appropriate string.

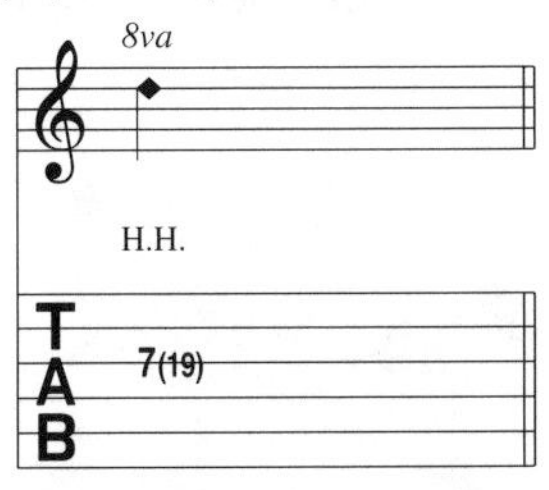

PICK SCRAPE: The edge of the pick is rubbed down (or up) the string, producing a scratchy sound.

MUFFLED STRINGS: A percussive sound is produced by laying the fret hand across the string(s) without depressing, and striking them with the pick hand.

PALM MUTING: The note is partially muted by the pick hand lightly touching the string(s) just before the bridge.

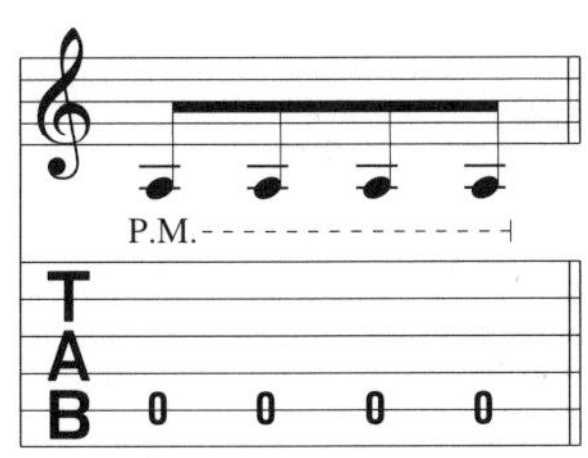

RAKE: Drag the pick across the strings indicated with a single motion.

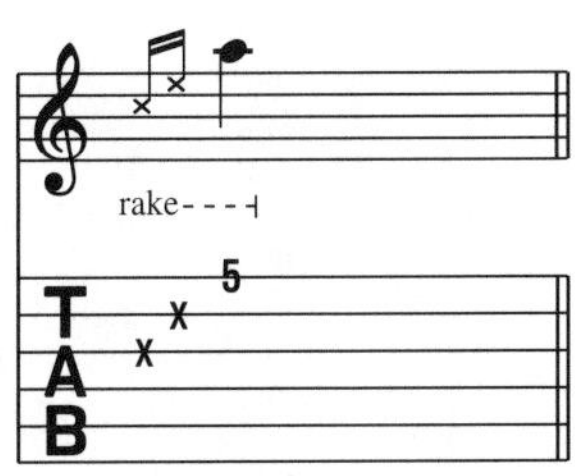

TREMOLO PICKING: The note is picked as rapidly and continuously as possible.

ARPEGGIATE: Play the notes of the chord indicated by quickly rolling them from bottom to top.

VIBRATO BAR DIVE AND RETURN: The pitch of the note or chord is dropped a specified number of steps (in rhythm) then returned to the original pitch.

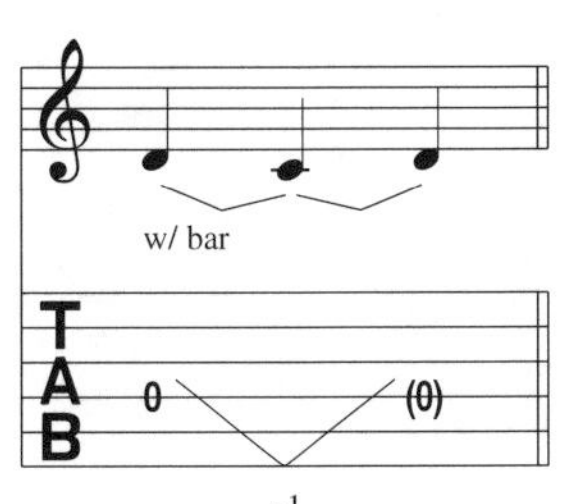

VIBRATO BAR SCOOP: Depress the bar just before striking the note, then quickly release the bar.

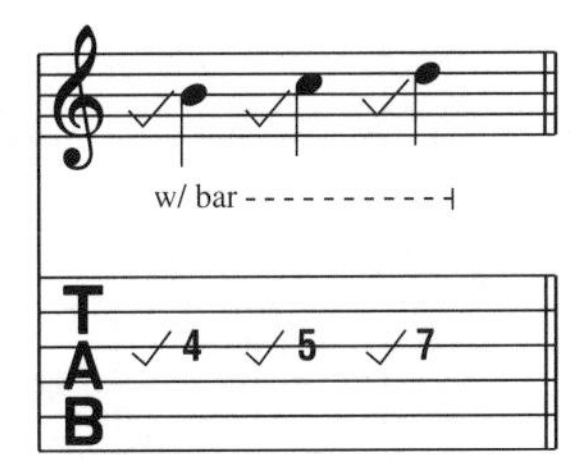

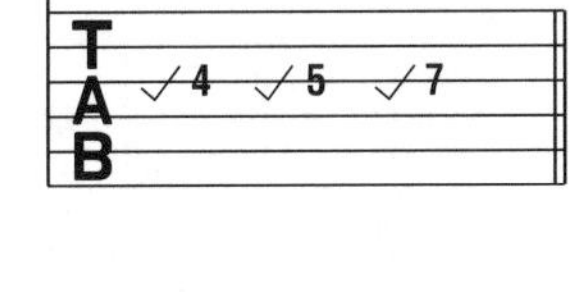

VIBRATO BAR DIP: Strike the note and then immediately drop a specified number of steps, then release back to the original pitch.

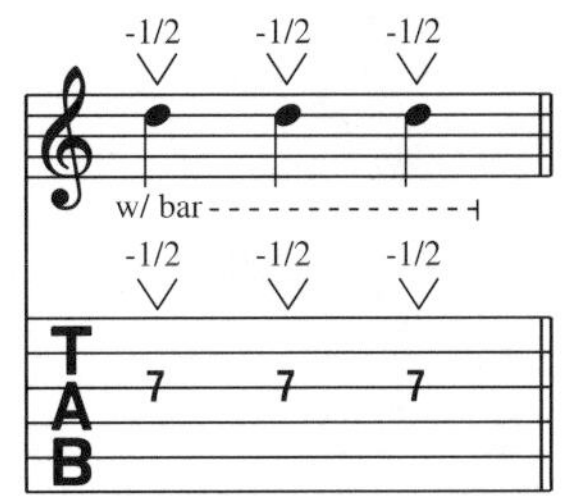

Additional Musical Definitions

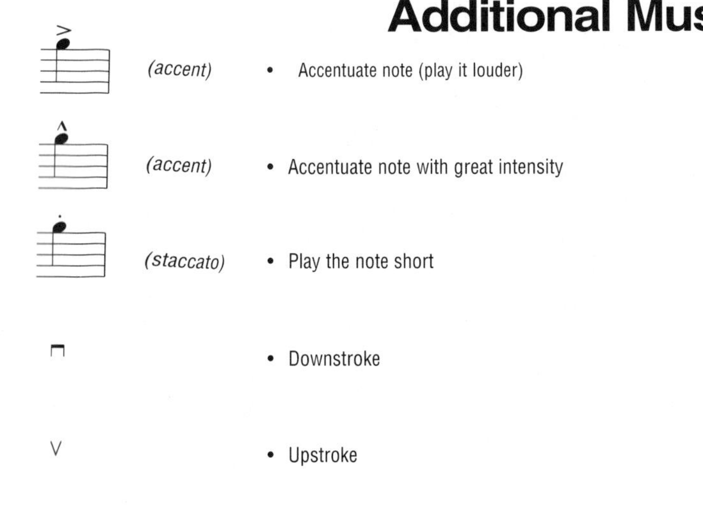

(accent) • Accentuate note (play it louder)

(accent) • Accentuate note with great intensity

(staccato) • Play the note short

• Downstroke

V • Upstroke

D.S. al Coda • Go back to the sign (𝄋), then play until the measure marked "***To Coda***," then skip to the section labelled "**Coda**."

D.C. al Fine • Go back to the beginning of the song and play until the measure marked "***Fine***" (end).

Rhy. Fig. • Label used to recall a recurring accompaniment pattern (usually chordal).

Riff • Label used to recall composed, melodic lines (usually single notes) which recur.

Fill • Label used to identify a brief melodic figure which is to be inserted into the arrangement.

Rhy. Fill • A chordal version of a Fill.

tacet • Instrument is silent (drops out).

• Repeat measures between signs.

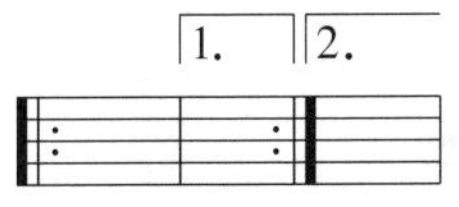

• When a repeated section has different endings, play the first ending only the first time and the second ending only the second time.

NOTE: Tablature numbers in parentheses mean:
1. The note is being sustained over a system (note in standard notation is tied), or
2. The note is sustained, but a new articulation (such as a hammer-on, pull-off, slide or vibrato begins), or
3. The note is a barely audible "ghost" note (note in standard notation is also in parentheses).

RECORDED VERSIONS GUITAR ®

RECORDED VERSIONS

The Best Note-For-Note Transcriptions Available

ALL BOOKS INCLUDE TABLATURE

00690501	Adams, Bryan – Greatest Hits	$19.95
00692015	Aerosmith – Greatest Hits	$22.95
00690488	Aerosmith – Just Push Play	$19.95
00690178	Alice in Chains – Acoustic	$19.95
00694865	Alice in Chains – Dirt	$19.95
00694925	Alice in Chains – Jar of Flies/Sap	$19.95
00690387	Alice in Chains – Nothing Safe – The Best of the Box	$19.95
00694932	Allman Brothers Band – Volume 1	$24.95
00694933	Allman Brothers Band – Volume 2	$24.95
00694934	Allman Brothers Band – Volume 3	$24.95
00690513	American Hi-Fi	$19.95
00694878	Atkins, Chet – Vintage Fingerstyle	$19.95
00690418	Audio Adrenaline, Best of	$17.95
00690366	Bad Company Original Anthology - Bk 1	$19.95
00690367	Bad Company Original Anthology - Bk 2	$19.95
00694929	Beatles: 1962-1966	$24.95
00694930	Beatles: 1967-1970	$24.95
00694880	Beatles – Abbey Road	$19.95
00690110	Beatles – Book 1 (White Album)	$19.95
00694832	Beatles – For Acoustic Guitar	$19.95
00660140	Beatles – Guitar Book	$19.95
00694863	Beatles – Sgt. Pepper's Lonely Hearts Club Band	$19.95
00690397	Beck – Midnite Vultures	$19.95
00694884	Benson, George – Best of	$19.95
00692385	Berry, Chuck	$19.95
00692200	Black Sabbath – We Sold Our Soul for Rock 'N' Roll	$19.95
00690305	Blink 182 – Dude Ranch	$19.95
00690389	Blink 182 – Enema of the State	$19.95
00690523	Blink 182 – Take Off Your Pants & Jacket	$19.95
00690028	Blue Oyster Cult – Cult Classics	$19.95
00690168	Buchanan, Roy – Collection	$19.95
00690491	Bowie, David – Best of	$19.95
00690451	Buckley, Jeff – Collection	$24.95
00690364	Cake – Songbook	$19.95
00690293	Chapman, Steven Curtis – Best of	$19.95
00690043	Cheap Trick – Best of	$19.95
00690171	Chicago – Definitive Guitar Collection	$22.95
00690415	Clapton Chronicles – Best of Eric Clapton	$18.95
00690393	Clapton, Eric – Selections from Blues	$19.95
00690074	Clapton, Eric – The Cream of Clapton	$24.95
00690010	Clapton, Eric – From the Cradle	$19.95
00660139	Clapton, Eric – Journeyman	$19.95
00694869	Clapton, Eric – Unplugged	$22.95
00694896	Clapton, Eric/John Mayall – Bluesbreakers	$19.95
00690162	Clash, Best of	$19.95
00690494	Coldplay – Parachutes	$19.95
00694940	Counting Crows – August & Everything After	$19.95
00694840	Cream – Disraeli Gears	$19.95
00690401	Creed – Human Clay	$19.95
00690352	Creed – My Own Prison	$19.95
00690484	dc Talk – Intermission: The Greatest Hits	$19.95
00690289	Deep Purple, Best of	$17.95
00690384	Di Franco, Ani – Best of	$19.95
00690322	Di Franco, Ani – Little Plastic Castle	$19.95
00690380	Di Franco, Ani – Up Up Up Up Up Up	$19.95
00695382	Dire Straits – Sultans of Swing	$19.95
00690347	Doors, The – Anthology	$22.95
00690348	Doors, The – Essential Guitar Collection	$16.95
00690524	Etheridge, Melissa – Skin	$19.95
00690349	Eve 6	$19.95
00690496	Everclear, Best of	$19.95
00690515	Extreme II – Pornograffitti	$19.95
00690323	Fastball – All the Pain Money Can Buy	$19.95
00690235	Foo Fighters – The Colour and the Shape	$19.95
00690394	Foo Fighters – There Is Nothing Left to Lose	$19.95
00690222	G3 Live – Satriani, Vai, Johnson	$22.95
00690536	Garbage – Beautiful Garbage	$19.95
00690438	Genesis Guitar Anthology	$19.95
00690338	Goo Goo Dolls – Dizzy Up the Girl	$19.95
00690114	Guy, Buddy – Collection Vol. A-J	$22.95
00690193	Guy, Buddy – Collection Vol. L-Y	$22.95
00694798	Harrison, George – Anthology	$19.95
00692930	Hendrix, Jimi – Are You Experienced?	$24.95
00692931	Hendrix, Jimi – Axis: Bold As Love	$22.95
00694944	Hendrix, Jimi – Blues	$24.95
00692932	Hendrix, Jimi – Electric Ladyland	$24.95
00690218	Hendrix, Jimi – First Rays of the New Rising Sun	$27.95
00690017	Hendrix, Jimi – Woodstock	$24.95
00660029	Holly, Buddy	$19.95
00690054	Hootie & The Blowfish – Cracked Rear View	$19.95
00690457	Incubus – Make Yourself	$19.95
00690544	Incubus – Morningview	$19.95
00690136	Indigo Girls – 1200 Curfews	$22.95
00694833	Joel, Billy – For Guitar	$19.95
00694912	Johnson, Eric – Ah Via Musicom	$19.95
00694799	Johnson, Robert – At the Crossroads	$19.95
00690271	Johnson, Robert – The New Transcriptions	$24.95
00699131	Joplin, Janis – Best of	$19.95
00693185	Judas Priest – Vintage Hits	$19.95
00690444	King, B.B. and Eric Clapton – Riding with the King	$19.95
00690339	Kinks, The – Best of	$19.95
00690279	Liebert, Ottmar + Luna Negra – Opium Highlights	$19.95
00694755	Malmsteen, Yngwie – Rising Force	$19.95
00694956	Marley, Bob – Legend	$19.95
00694945	Marley, Bob – Songs of Freedom	$24.95
00690283	McLachlan, Sarah – Best of	$19.95
00690382	McLachlan, Sarah – Mirrorball	$19.95
00690442	Matchbox 20 – Mad Season	$19.95
00690239	Matchbox 20 – Yourself or Someone Like You	$19.95
00694952	Megadeth – Countdown to Extinction	$19.95
00690391	Megadeth – Risk	$19.95
00694951	Megadeth – Rust in Peace	$22.95
00690495	Megadeth – The World Needs a Hero	$19.95
00690040	Miller, Steve, Band – Greatest Hits	$19.95
00690448	MxPx – The Ever Passing Moment	$19.95
00690189	Nirvana – From the Muddy Banks of the Wishkah	$19.95
00694913	Nirvana – In Utero	$19.95
00694883	Nirvana – Nevermind	$19.95
00690026	Nirvana – Unplugged™ in New York	$19.95
00690121	Oasis – (What's the Story) Morning Glory	$19.95
00690358	Offspring, The – Americana	$19.95
00690485	Offspring, The – Conspiracy of One	$19.95
00690203	Offspring, The – Smash	$18.95
00694847	Osbourne, Ozzy – Best of	$22.95
00694830	Osbourne, Ozzy – No More Tears	$19.95
00690538	Oysterhead – The Grand Pecking Order	$19.95
00694855	Pearl Jam – Ten	$19.95
00690439	Perfect Circle, A – Mer De Noms	$19.95
00690176	Phish – Billy Breathes	$22.95
00690424	Phish – Farmhouse	$19.95
00690240	Phish – Hoist	$19.95
00690331	Phish – Story of the Ghost	$19.95
00690428	Pink Floyd – Dark Side of the Moon	$19.95
00690456	P.O.D. – The Fundamental Elements of Southtown	$19.95
00693864	Police, The – Best of	$19.95
00690299	Presley, Elvis – Best of Elvis: The King of Rock 'n' Roll	$19.95
00694975	Queen – Greatest Hits	$24.95
00694910	Rage Against the Machine	$19.95
00690395	Rage Against the Machine – The Battle of Los Angeles	$19.95
00690145	Rage Against the Machine – Evil Empire	$19.95
00690478	Rage Against the Machine – Renegades	$19.95
00690426	Ratt – Best of	$19.95
00690055	Red Hot Chili Peppers – Bloodsugarsexmagik	$19.95
00690379	Red Hot Chili Peppers – Californication	$19.95
00690090	Red Hot Chili Peppers – One Hot Minute	$22.95
00694899	R.E.M. – Automatic for the People	$19.95
00690014	Rolling Stones – Exile on Main Street	$24.95
00690135	Rush, Otis – Collection	$19.95
00690502	Saliva – Every Six Seconds	$19.95
00690031	Santana's Greatest Hits	$19.95
00120123	Shepherd, Kenny Wayne – Trouble Is	$19.95
00690419	Slipknot	$19.95
00690530	Slipknot – Iowa	$19.95
00690330	Social Distortion – Live at the Roxy	$19.95
00690385	Sonicflood	$19.95
00694957	Stewart, Rod – Unplugged...And Seated	$22.95
00690021	Sting – Fields of Gold	$19.95
00690519	Sum 41 – All Killer No Filler	$19.95
00690425	System of a Down	$19.95
00690531	System of a Down – Toxicity	$19.95
00694824	Taylor, James – Best of	$16.95
00690238	Third Eye Blind	$19.95
00690403	Third Eye Blind – Blue	$19.95
00690295	Tool – Aenima	$19.95
00690039	Vai, Steve – Alien Love Secrets	$24.95
00690343	Vai, Steve – Flex-able Leftovers	$19.95
00660137	Vai, Steve – Passion & Warfare	$24.95
00690392	Vai, Steve – The Ultra Zone	$19.95
00690370	Vaughan, Stevie Ray and Double Trouble – The Real Deal: Greatest Hits Volume 2	$22.95
00690455	Vaughan, Stevie Ray – Blues at Sunrise	$19.95
00690116	Vaughan, Stevie Ray – Guitar Collection	$24.95
00660136	Vaughan, Stevie Ray – In Step	$19.95
00660058	Vaughan, Stevie Ray – Lightnin' Blues 1983-1987	$24.95
00690417	Vaughan, Stevie Ray – Live at Carnegie Hall	$19.95
00694835	Vaughan, Stevie Ray – The Sky Is Crying	$22.95
00690015	Vaughan, Stevie Ray – Texas Flood	$19.95
00120026	Walsh, Joe – Look What I Did...	$24.95
00694789	Waters, Muddy – Deep Blues	$24.95
00690071	Weezer	$19.95
00690516	Weezer (The Green Album)	$19.95
00690286	Weezer – Pinkerton	$19.95
00690447	Who, The – Best of	$24.95
00690320	Williams, Dar – Best of	$17.95
00690319	Wonder, Stevie – Some of the Best	$17.95
00690443	Zappa, Frank – Hot Rats	$19.95